THE GRAND MATCHES
OF CRICKET
PLAYED IN ENGLAND
FROM 1771 TO 1791

THE GRAND MATCHES OF CRICKET PLAYED IN ENGLAND FROM 1771 TO 1791

ARRANGED AND PRINTED
BY W. EPPS

WITH AN INTRODUCTION
BY
DAVID RAYVERN ALLEN

Published by J.W. McKenzie 1989

This book was originally published in Rochester in 1799. It is here reprinted in exact facsimile with the addition of a new Introduction.

ISBN 0-947821-01-5

Printed by
E. & E. Plumridge Ltd, Linton, Cambridge.

INTRODUCTION

For those of a certain age with a leaning towards nostalgia and whose hearing is perhaps not what it was, mention of Troy Town could well conjure up memories of cherished 'Children's Hours' with the Mayor and Mr. Grouser, sir! Whereas, however, Toy Town was a figment of S.G. Hulme Beaman's imagination, Troy Town is a very real district of the cathedral city of Rochester-upon-Medway in Kent. It was there, in King Street, during the late 18th and early 19th centuries, that one William Epps ran his printing press.

Today, a few parts of Troy Town still retain distinctive elements that Epps would recognise, especially visible around the corner of Union Street and East Row where resided the eminent wine merchant, John Cazeneuve Troy, who gave his name to the area after letting land for building leases. Troy Town was erected in the first half of the nineteenth century, and consisted of 'a large cluster of neat and substantially-built houses, occupying about four principal streets interspersed with eleven or so less spacious thoroughfares containing small artisan dwellings' which became, intrinsically, one of the operative sectors of Rochester. Early this century, a local newspaper described the place as 'scruffy and unmade', though it was not until 1963 and '64 that demolition on a large scale made way for so-called development, mainly high-rise flats and council properties.

William Epps was politically oriented, with aspirations at both local and national level and coincidentally, in view of the first paragraph, he at one time became embroiled in a contest for the office of Mayor of the City. Epps produced a number of political pamphlets and judging from the criticisms to be found therein, he was a man of strong views with a zealous social conscience; probably of a somewhat choleric nature, impetuous and yet certainly not lacking courage.† He readily admitted to being a controversial character and susceptible to errors of judgement, however, there is no doubt that he would have gained a good measure of popular support for his stands against what he saw as political chicanery and injustice. Epps used the power of the printed word, literally at his elbow, to castigate a lot of his opponents and, not unexpectedly, much umbrage resulted from his stout defence, if not active pursuit, of a thicker-than-thin line of acrimony against those with much to lose. Even his own solicitor, in an unguarded momentduring a liquid luncheon, was moved to declare; "Damn his old eyes, a few months imprisonment would do him good, he ought to have been hanged years ago!"

So, what encouraged Epps to venture into the gentler pastures of cricket and compile a collection of scores? There is little doubt he was a practitioner of the game and it is most probably he who is found in Britcher's Scores for 1799 having on Saturday, July 20th of that year taken part in what is described as 'a grand single match of cricket in Marsh's new ground, near the Royal George, at Rochester, between two gentlemen of Troy-Town, against two gentlemen of Rochester, for 50 guineas.' Epps, on that day, was representing Rochester in tandem with a player called Bishop, who, in fact, came from Stroud. Their opponents were Messrs. Lamb and Marsh.

In the first innings Epps scored 4 runs from 29 balls received, 19 of which he had managed to hit, before being bowled by Marsh. In the second innings, he lasted a mere five balls before again falling victim to Marsh, this time for a duck. Epps, however, later upstaged the proprietor of the ground by catching him for a single, to bring the match to a triumphant conclusion for the Rochester pair by 2 runs. The starting price against them had been 6 to 4.

Almost certainly, Epps was acquainted with or had, at least, met Samuel Britcher, scorer for M.C.C., maybe on that very day in 1799. A discussion between them could have motivated Epps to collate details of matches preceding the period of the Britcher Scores. As can be seen, Epps starts his 'Apology' with *the following is a collection of all the principal Matches which were played from the year 1771 down to 1791, from which time there has been a regular annual publication, by Mr. Britcher, the scorer to the Mary-le-bone Club, which, of course, obviates the necessity of continuing this publication to a subsequent period.*

On the other hand, even though it is tempting to speculate that this was the case, with Epps' publication being issued in the same year, 1799, it is more than possible that the idea had been in his mind for some time.

As he observes, the scores *'are carefully corrected from the collections of several Gentlemen, none of which have ever been published'*. The actual process of gathering together and re-copying the manuscripts of such worthies as the Duke of Dorset, their noble Lords Tankerville and Winchilsea, Sir Horatio Mann and Squire Paulet would take no little while. It is a fair assumption that one or two, if not all of these gentry, provided some source material – Mann, for instance, was known to take pencil notes at matches.

Another thought, is that by associating himself, however tenuously, with members of the aristocracy Epps was helping to promote his social and political ambitions: he obtained by purchase the freedom of the City of Rochester in 1802 and twice stood in a poll to select Members of Parliament.

The book, itself, is of major importance to cricket antiquarians. Excepting the long-lost printed book of scores of the old Hambledon Club, Epps is the earliest widespread coverage of cricket of the time in a book wholly devoted to the game. Notwithstanding, A.J. Gaston's disparaging comment in the *Cricket Field* of 1893, where he determines that *'several important matches are omitted from this book, which is not at all valuable'*, subsequent history has happily decided otherwise. A.D. Taylor, Gaston's contemporary and fellow bibliographer, gives a quite differerent perspective when contradicting his friend in his invaluable *Catalogue of Cricket Literature, 1906:*

'Many important matches are omitted from this publication, which, however, is a gem to collectors. Mr. Haygarth informed Mr. Ashley-Cooper that, but for this book, vol. 1 of Cricket Scores and Biographies would not have been nearly as complete as it is. It was almost at the last moment and quite by accident that Mr. Haygarth obtained a copy of this work. Worth at least from 20s to 30s.

Having appeared in cricket's two bibliographies (Gaston and Taylor), Epps completed the hat-trick with J.W. Goldman's opus in 1937. *'One of the scarcest cricket items. Should fetch £10 to £20'* was the ace collectors' assessment.

When writing an article on the Goldman library in *The Cricketer* of December 1965, Irving Rosenwater rightly refers to a copy of Epps as being *'almost unprocurable'*. In the Hodgson auction of the first portion of the Goldman collection at Chancery Lane, London, in November 1966, his copy of the book was sold to Epworths for £50. The importance and rarity of the volume was recognised by a full page illustration in the catalogue. The present writer cannot recall having seen another copy listed in post-war catalogues though it may well have happened; no doubt the very few that appear to exist have changed hands privately or been snapped up from dealers before being displayed publicly.

How many copies are extant? It is an impossible question to answer accurately, though there may well be no more than half-a-dozen.

John Arlott acquired a copy of Epps for his cricket library from Leslie Gutteridge many years ago, as a memento of his father, and the fly-leaf is suitably inscribed, 'William John Arlott, 1886–1959'. Another Epps is owned by John McKenzie, the publisher of this volume – this was once in the possession of J.W. Goldman and later bought by C.S. Cheshire. A third copy is in the Lord's' library and there is another thought to reside abroad. Conceivably, there are further Epps' to be found in libraries or in private hands, possibly owned by individuals for whom a book on cricket has no special attraction.

What of the book, as such? The matches covered within are naturally congregated in the cricketing heartland of the time, mainly Kent and Hampshire with nods towards London, Middlesex and Surrey. We find evocative venues, such as Bourne Paddock, Broad-Halfpenny, Moulsey Hurst and Laleham Burway housing county sides and elevens labelled 'All-England', as well as teams gathered under the patronage of nobility and gentleman.

Epps starts with a couple of 'remarkable occurrences' and a game at the Artillery Ground in 1772 and finishes, appropriately enough, at Marylebone in 1790 with the dawn of a new era. This is the match in which the legendary David Harris bowled Hampshire to a convincing victory over a national side. On that last page there is an errata note, though Epps obviously saw fit to leave untouched the several spelling variants that occur throughout his collection: these, in fact, do not jar, rather do they charmingly enhance the flavour of the period.

Our awareness of the rudiments surrounding cricket two hundred years ago is also heightened by the rider on 'a tye game' at Windmill Downs in 1783. A dispute over the result, principally caused by the fallibility of notching runs on a stick, is a reminder that it was to be very few years before the practise became obsolete and the pen reigned supreme.

As we glance through the scores, the deeds of familiar and less familiar names propel us inexorably, as if in a time-warp, towards rural downlands where rustic figures in cotton smocks and members of 'The Fancy' in frock-coats together battled for supremacy with bat and ball. Those gladiatorial contests capture our imagination as much today as surely they did for the spectators and players who watched and took part.

It would seem that William Epps died, aged 68, in 1833 (the scrawled writing on the register viewed via microfilm is hard to decipher) and was buried on November 9th at St. Nicholas Church near the Castle, the very year when Nyren's classic 'Young Cricketer's Tutor' brought a new insight of the early days of the game. If that was indeed the case, it provided the kind of linked inheritance that cricket's *afficionados* have bestowed throughout its existence. From one hand, the facts and statistics - from another, the comment and romance. Thank heavens, William Epps helped preserve a record for posterity.

† Footnote

A few of these pamphlets, including one or two which contained incendiary comment triggering threats of prosecution, are held at the County Library, Northgate, Rochester.

a) TRUTH UNMASKED; or, A True Delineation of Circumstances attending the late Extraordinary Contest, for the representation of The City of Rochester... 1806

b) AN ALPHABETICAL LIST OF THE FREEMEN OF THE CITY OF ROCHESTER... 1807

c) PROCEEDINGS OF A SELECT COMMITTEE of the House of Commons... 1808

d) ANTIDOTE TO ELECTIONEERING CALUMNY; or, An Historical Narrative of the late Memorable Contest for the Representation of the City of Rochester... 1817

e) CITY OF ROCHESTER Rules and Regulations, for the Supporting and Maintaining a Society, called the Freemens' Club 1818

f) SOME PLAIN FACTS, addressed to The People of Rochester... 1819

CRICKET.

A

COLLECTION

OF ALL

THE GRAND MATCHES

OF

CRICKET,

PLAYED IN ENGLAND,

WITHIN TWENTY YEARS;

VIZ.

FROM 1771, TO 1791,

NEVER BEFORE PUBLISHED.

ARRANGED, AND PRINTED,

BY W. EPPS,

TROY-TOWN, ROCHESTER.

1799.

APOLOGY.

The following is a collection of all the principal Matches which were played from the year 1771 down to 1791, from which time there has been a regular annual publication, by Mr. Britcher, the Scorer to the Mary-le-bone Club, which, of course, obviates the necessity of continuing this publication to a subsequent period.

Some few of the earliest Matches are imperfect, so far as relates to putting out the Players, which is principally owing to the method of scoring at that time; but in other respects they are carefully corrected from the collections of several Gentlemen, none of which have ever been published.

This collection being highly interesting to the Amateurs in the Game, as well as to those whose names are recorded as eminent players, will, no doubt, be by them esteemed a choice treasure.

CRICKET.

REMARKABLE OCCURRENCES.

A moſt ſingular circumſtance, we are informed, attended a game at Cricket very lately at Hadlow; three pariſhes joined to play with Hadlow, who put out the whole eleven of their adverſaries for only four runs. *Kentiſh Gazette.*

Canterbury Journal, July 8, 1783.

On the 18th ult. a game at Cricket was played between Brightling and Netherfield, in Suſſex, in the courſe of which it is remarkable, that one man on the ſide of Netherfield fetched as many notches at one ſtroke, as all the Brightling gameſters did their firſt innings, being ſix only: their ſecond innings added but 23 to their firſt, making in the whole 29. The Netherfield people headed them 113, both the innings amounting to 142.

ARTILLERY GROUND,

1772,

Five of Kent, againſt Five of Hampſhire.

HAMPSHIRE.	1ſt inn.	2d inn.	KENT.	1ſt inn.	2d inn
Small	4	6	Boreman	0	2
Suter	1	0	R. May	1	7
Lear	1	7	Minſhall	26	11
Brett	0	4	Miller	0	2
Nyren	5	29	Frame not out	8	1
	11	46		35	23

Kent won by one wicket.

BOURNE PADDOCK,

August 19, 1772,

Hambleton Club, (with Yalden & Edmeads) *against all England.*

ALL ENGLAND.

	1st inn.	2d inn.
Lumpy	14	12
Richard May	3	0
Wood	0	20
Pattenden	20	4
Minshall	24	9
Simmons	3	1
Fuggles	0	1
Miller	14	17
White	8	5
Palmer	29	14
Boreman	0	2
Byes	21	16
	136	101

HAMBLETON CLUB.

	1st inn.	2d inn.
Brett	11	0
Suter	26	11
Lear	29	7
Small	22	48
Buckstewart	13	12
Ridge, Esq.	4	8
Barber	0	2
Hogsflesh	0	1
Yalden	4	1
Edmeads	7	4
Curry	0	6
Byes	7	13
	123	113

ARTILLERY GROUND,

1773.

Hampshire, against all England.

HAMPSHIRE.

	1st inn.	2d inn.
Brett	1 b May	6 b Lumpy
Nyren	4 b Lumpy	4 b ditto
Small	2 b May	7 b May
Suter	1 b ditto	3 c Miller
Lear	16 run out	13 c Minshall
	24	33

ALL ENGLAND.

	1st inn.	2d inn.
R. May	1	0
Lumpy	9	8 b Nyren
Minshall	15	7
Miller	5 b Brett	11 not out
Palmer	1	1
	31	27

LALEHAM BURWAY,
1773.

Kent against Surry, with four Gentlemen on each side.

KENT.	1st inn.	2d inn.	SURRY.	1st inn.	2d inn.
Duke of Dorset	14	6	Ld. Tankerville	15	2
Sir Hor. Mann	1	8	Stone	35	2
Davis	23	4	Lewis	2	9
Hussey	7	9	Hon. De Burgh	0	0
Miller	4	18	Edmeads	11	0
Pattenden	25	4	Yalden	9	0
Booker	2	4	Lumpy	10	11
Newman	28	0	Wood	3	6
Fuggles	3	6	White	44	23
T. May	20	10	Palmer	8	5
Wheeler	1	0	Francis	30	9
Byes	5	8	Byes	8	3
	133	77		175	70

ARTILLERY GROUND,
1773.

Hampshire, (with Yalden) *against all England.*

HAMPSHIRE.	1st inn.	2d inn.	ALL ENGLAND.	1st inn.	2d inn.
Brett	1	14	Lumpy	5	
Nyren	0	14	Frame	11	
Suter	29	32	Wood	15	
Small	58	25	Child	38	
Aylward	8	1	White	24	1
Hogsflesh	2	14	Colchin	1	9
Buckfteward	10	5	Boreman	5	55
Yalden	4	2	Wood of Seal	5	
Curry	0	3	Bullen	1	1
Barber	15	25	Read	13	
Lear	0	3	Palmer	52	30
Byes	5	16	Byes	17	4
	132	154		187	100

All England won by 5 wickets.

SEVENOAKS,

1773.

Hampſhire, (with Yalden) *againſt All England.*

HAMPSHIRE.

	1ſt inn.		2d inn.	
Brett	26	b Lumpy	1	c Minſhall
Lear	14	run out	15	not out
Suter	11	b Lumpy	9	c Lumpy
Buckſteward	5	run out	0	b Wood
Yalden	5	b Wood	0	b Lumpy
Aylward	4	c Minſhall	13	b ditto
Hogsfleſh	4	c Simmons	0	c Wood
Small	3	c Lumpy	4	run out
Nyren	2	c White	5	c Minſhall
Curry	2	not out	2	b Lumpy
Barber	1	b R. May	0	b Wood
Byes	0	Byes	0	
	77		49	

ALL ENGLAND.

	1ſt inn.		2d inn.
Miller	73	c Barber	
Simmons	20	b Brett	
T. May	16	b Barber	
Minſhall	15	hit his own wicket	
Wood, of Seal	14	b Hogsfleſh	
Wood, of Surry	12	b ditto	
R May	10	not out	
White	7	b Nyren	
Pattenden	1	c Hogsfleſh	
Lumpy	6	b Brett	
Child	1	b Hogsfleſh	
Byes	2		
	177		

All England won by one innings, and 51 runs.

BOURNE PADDOCK,

1773.

Surry against Kent, with four Gentlemen on each Side.

SURRY.

	1st inn.		2d. inn.	
L. Tankerville	0	b May	3	c Davis
Bartholomew	3	c Simmons	10	b Miller
Lewis	0	b the Duke	21	not out
Stone	12	b ditto	24	b Miller
Lumpy	6	b Miller	8	b ditto
Wood	6	c Sir H. Mann	6	c R. May
Palmer	22	c Davis	38	c the Duke
White	5	b the Duke	60	c Hussey
Yalden	17	not out	1	b the Duke
Child	0	b May	3	b ditto
Francis	5	b the Duke	36	c Wood
Byes	1	Byes	7	
	77		217	

KENT.

	1st inn.		2d inn.	
Duke of Dorset	25	b Wood	1	b Wood
Sir H. Mann	3	b ditto	22	c Ld. Tankerville
Davis	4	b ditto	0	c Lewis
Hussey	0	not out	0	b Wood
Miller	13	c Yalden	10	run out
Simmons	5	b Lumpy	4	c Yalden
R. May	0	b Wood	0	not out
T. May	4	b Lumpy	5	c Child
Louch	5	c Stone	26	b Lumpy
Pattenden	0	c Lewis	1	b ditto
Wood, of Seal	1	c Wood	9	c Bartholomew
Byes	3	Byes	0	
	63		78	

B

Surry won by 153 runs.

BROAD-HALFPENNY,

1773.

Hampſhire, (with Francis) *againſt all England.*

HAMPSHIRE.

	1ſt inn.		2d inn.	
Ridge	0	b the Duke	24	c Yalden
Hogsfleſh	6	b Lumpy	0	b Duke
Purchaſe	1	b ditto	17	c Miller
Small	16	b ditto	22	run out
Suter	2	b Duke	39	b Duke
Nyren	5	b ditto	6	not out
Lear	2	b ditto	13	c Simmons
Francis	2	b Wood	6	c Palmer
Davis	30	run out	7	b Lumpy
Barber	2	not out	1	b ditto
Aylward	18	b Lumpy	4	b ditto
Byes	5	Byes	1	
	89		140	

ALL ENGLAND.

	1ſt inn.		2d inn.	
Stone	0	b Hogsfleſh		
Palmer	68	c Ridge		
Minſhall	11	c ditto		
White	69	b Purchaſe		
Miller	18	b Hogsfleſh		
Duke of Dorſet	3	c Barber		
Yalden	0	b Purchaſe	10	not out
Simmons	3	c Nyren	13	c Hogsfleſh
Pattenden	1	b Purchaſe	4	not out
Lumpy	1	b ditto		
Wood	17	not out		
Byes	11	Byes	1	
	202		28	

England won by 9 wickets. Simmons got ſeven runs at one hit.

SEVENOAKS,

1773.

Kent, (with Minſhall) *againſt Surry.*

SURRY.

	1ſt inn.		2d inn.	
Wood	16	c Simmons	5	b Frame
Palmer	20	run out	20	c Simmons
White	59	c Wood	0	c Minſhall
Francis	14	b Fiſh	9	b Frame
Ld. Tankerville	12	b the Duke	18	c ditto
Yalden	8	b Booker	3	b Duke
Phillips	14	c Miller	3	c Simmons
Childs	0	run out	8	b Duke
Page	2	b Booker	1	c Minſhall
Lumpy	8	not out	0	b Frame
Blake	8	b Booker	0	not out
Byes	9	Byes	3	
	170		70	

KENT.

	1ſt inn.		2d inn.	
Louch	0	c Phillips	0	c Francis
Wood	36	b Lumpy	5	not out
Minſhall	21	c Yalden	32	c Page
Miller	42	b Frances	32	not out
Duke of Dorſet	14	c Yalden	23	b White
Simmons	0	b Wood	6	c Palmer
Booker	0	c ditto		
Newman	1	b ditto		
Frame	6	c White		
Fiſh	14	c Frances		
Pattenden	1	not out		
Byes	6	Byes	2	
	141		100	

Kent won by 7 wickets.

LALEHAM BURWAY,

1773.

September 16, 17, & 18,

Hampshire, (with Francis & Bailey) *against Surry*, (with Miller & Minshall.)

HAMPSHIRE.

	1st inn.		2d inn.	
Aylward	11	b Francis	36	c Field
Brett	0	b Wood	8	b Wood
Small	0	b ditto	3	c Yalden
Suter	13	b Francis	19	b White
Lear	0	c Ld. Tankerville	17	c Minshall
Bayley	4	b Lumpy	19	b White
Stewart	8	c Francis	10	run ont
Davis	0	c Ld. Tankerv.	4	c Ld. Tankerv.
Purchase	1	b Wood	8	b Lumpy
Hogsflesh	0	not out	6	not out
Frame	0	b Francis	12	c White
Byes	1	Byes	3	
	38		145	

SURRY.

	1st inn.		2d inn.	
Palmer	6	b Brett		
Wood	7	c Stewart		
Miller	37	b Frame	30	not out
White	17	c Small	10	not out
Minshall	29	c Purchase		
Ld. Tankerville	0	b Hogsflesh	3	b Brett
Francis	4	b Frame		
Yalden	0	c Suter		
Lumpy	11	c Stewart		
Field	4	not out		
Childs	0	c Bayley	18	c Brett
Byes	5	Byes	3	
	120		64	

Surry won by 8 wickets.

SEVENOAKS,

1774.

July 8, & 9,

Hampshire, (with Lumpy) *against all England.*

HAMPSHIRE.

	1st inn.		2d inn.	
Aylward	29	run out	61	c Minshall
Francis	4	b Bullen	1	b Wood
Small	10	b ditto	20	run out
Suter	12	c ditto	30	b Bullen
Lear	28	b Frame	14	b Wood
Nyren	10	b Bullen	18	c Minshall
Stewart	14	not out	7	b Colchin
Lumpy	21	c Wood, of Surry	11	b ditto
Curry	8	b Bullen	7	b Wood
Brett	2	b ditto	4	not out
Purchase	0	c White	0	b Colchin
Byes	1	Byes	9	
	139		182	

ALL ENGLAND.

	1st inn.		2d inn.	
Ld. Tankerville	1	c Small	5	b Lumpy
Stone	0	c ditto	3	b Brett
Bullen	7	b Lumpy	1	b Lumpy
Minshall	6	c Purchase	8	b ditto
Miller	16	b Nyren	12	c Suter
Colchin	10	not out	19	c Lear
White	17	b Brett	4	c Nyren
Palmer	3	c Small	5	b Lumpy
Wood, of Seal	27	b Nyren	3	c Brett
Frame	1	b Brett	3	b Purchase
Wood	0	b Lumpy	0	not out
Byes	0	Byes	1	
	88		64	

Hampshire won by 169 runs.

GUILDFORD,

1774.

July 20,——a Plate of 50*l.* to the winners.

Hampſhire, againſt Surry (with Miller.)

HAMPSHIRE.

	1ſt inn.		2d inn.	
Francis	8	c Field	14	b Wood
Aylward	13	b Wood	5	c Lumpy
Small	28	c Muggeridge	10	b ditto
Suter	11	run out	10	not out
Lear	0	b Wood	9	not out
Nyren	10	b Lumpy		
Stewart	5	b White		
Brett	2	b ditto		
Hogsfleſh	0	c Yalden		
Curry	6	not out		
Purchaſe	7	b White		
Byes	1			
	91		48	

SURRY.

	1ſt inn.		2d inn.	
R. Miller	3	c Curry	2	c Nyren
J. Miller	3	b Brett	1	b ditto
White	13	c Nyren	1	b Brett
Palmer	26	not out	2	b Francis
Muggeridge	0	b Nyren	0	b Nyren
Field	3	b Brett	16	b Brett
Lumpy	3	b Hogsfleſh	13	not out
Wood	0	b Brett	7	b Brett
Yalden	0	b ditto	8	b Francis
Quiddenden	3	b Hogsfleſh	10	b ditto
Edmeads	5	b Brett	10	b Brett
Byes	2	Byes	7	
	61		77	

Hampſhire won by 7 wickets.

SEVENOAKS,
1774.
Auguſt 8 & 9,

Kent (with three men given) *againſt Hampſhire.*

HAMPSHIRE.

	1ſt inn.		2d inn.	
Aylward	1	b the Duke	17	run out
Curry	9	b Lumpy	26	b Lumpy
Small	18	b ditto	55	not out
Suter	0	c Waller	12	c Waller
Nyren	3	c Simmons	3	b Booker
Lear	4	c White	8	b ditto
Brett	1	c Bullen	11	c Lumpy
Francis	3	b Lumpy	8	b Bullen
Ridge	2	b ditto	1	c Simmons
Purchaſe	1	c Booker	11	c Colchin
Hogsfleſh	3	not out	3	b White
Byes	1	Byes	4	
	46		159	

KENT.

	1ſt inn.		2d inn.
Duke of Dorſet	77	c Small	
Miller	95	c Purchaſe	
Colchin	0	b Brett	
Simmons	1	b ditto	
Walker	2	b Nyren	
White	0	b Hogsfleſh	
Pattenden	24	b Francis	
Brazier	0	run out	
Booker	22	c Brett	
Lumpy	7	c Aylward	
Bullen	8	not out	
Byes	4		
	240		

Kent won by one innings, and 35 runs.

BROAD-HALFPENNY,

1774.

Auguſt 15,

Kent, (with three men given (*againſt Hampſhire*.

HAMPSHIRE.

	1ſt inn.		2d. inn.	
Ridge	1	c Brazier	8	b White
Small	45	c ditto	8	c Waller
Suter	3	b Lumpy	9	c Bullen
Lear	14	b ditto	0	b White
Nyren	35	b Colchin	20	b Colchin
Aylward	30	b Lumpy	4	c ditto
Stewart	7	b Booker	5	b Lumpy
Curry	20	c Colchin	33	c the Duke
Brett	0	c ditto	8	b Colchin
Francis	14	not out	22	run out
Barber	0	c Simmons	5	not out
Byes	5	Byes	7	
	174		129	

KENT.

	1ſt inn.		2d inn.	
Duke of Dorſet	5	b Brett		
Waller	6	b ditto		
Simmons	6	not out	4	b Hogsfleſh
Lumpy	3	b Barber		
Miller	40	c Brett	45	c Hogsfleſh
Colchin	25	b Barber	1	not out
White	1	b Curry	50	b Brett
Pattenden	35	c Small	14	b Nyren
Brazier	4	b Nyren	5	not out
Booker	7	c ditto	3	run out
Bullen	27	b Brett	2	b Nyren
Byes	9	Byes	12	
	168		136	

Kent won by 4 wickets.

ARTILLERY GROUND,
1774.

A mixed Match.

	1ſt inn.		2d inn.	
Boreman	0	b R. May	2	b R. May
Colchin	29	b ditto	17	b ditto
Minſhall	20	b ditto	1	b Wood
Read	0	b ditto	15	b ditto
Bullen	0	c Wood, of Seal	0	b ditto
Byes	1	Byes	2	
	50		37	

	1ſt inn.		2b inn.	
T. May	6	b Read	2	run out
R. May	1	b Colchin	6	b Bullen
Wood, of Seal	6	b ditto	0	b ditto
Wood, of Surry	0	b ditto	1	b ditto
Miller	6	b ditto	7	b Read
Byes	1	Byes	2	
	20		18	

LALEHAM BURWAY,
1774.

Hampſhire, (with Lumpy) *againſt all England.*

HAMPSHIRE.	1ſt inn.	2d inn.
Curry	9	
Small	47	
Lumpy	22	
Lear	12	
Suter	67	
Nyren	21	
Aylward	37	
Francis	29	
Stewart	11	
Purchaſe	37	
Brett	9	
Byes	6	
	307	

ALL-ENGLAND.	1ſt inn.	2d inn.
D. of Dorſet	19	6
L. Tankerv.	18	35
Stone	14	4
Minſhall	37	38
May	7	6
Miller	3	26
Wood	10	0
White	5	0
Palmer	0	6
Childs	2	6
Yalden	1	0
Byes	6	6
	122	133

ARTILLERY GROUND,

May 22, & 23, 1775.

Hampshire, (with White) *against Kent*, (with Lumpey)

KENT.

	1st inn.	2d inn.
Bullen	7 b White	56 b Brett
Booker	8 b Brett	35 b ditto
Miller	3 b ditto	3 b ditto
Lumpy	6 b White	8 b White
Brazier	13 b Brett	0 b Brett
	37	102

HAMPSHIRE.

	1st inn.	2d inn.
Small	75 b Lumpy	14 not out
White	0 b ditto	1 b Lumpy
Brett	4 b ditto	14 b ditto
Suter	0 b ditto	15 b ditto
Lear	13 b ditto	4 c Booker
	92	48

BROAD-HALFPENNY,

July 13.

Hampshire, (D. Dorset) *ag. Surry* (with Miller & Minshall)

	1st inn.	2d inn.		1st inn.	2d inn.
Duke of Dorset	8	6	L. Tankerv.	2	11
Small	38	136	Miller	15	0
Francis	45	0	Palmer	0	22
Suter	6	0	White	7	0
Lear	21	2	Minshall	7	0
Nyren	12	98	Yalden	26	27
Aylward	1	2	Wood	29	0
Barber	9	30	Field	49	15
Brett	19	68	Lumpy	4	0
Curry	0	7	Edmeads	6	0
Taylor	8	1	Quiddenden	2	0
Byes	1	7	Byes	4	3
	136	357		151	78

Hampshire won by 296 runs.

SEVENOAKS,
1775.

Kent, (with two men) *againſt Hampſhire.*

June 14, & 15.

HAMPSHIRE.

	1ſt inn.		2d inn.	
Ridge	4	b Booker	0	b Lumpy
Francis	1	c Simmons	1	b May
Small	3	b Lumpy	14	c Simmons
Suter	15	c Bullen	5	b Lumpy
Lear	27	c Miller	2	c Bullen
Nyren	11	b White	3	b Lumpy
Aylward	38	b Lumpy	0	b ditto
Hogsfleſh	7	run out	3	not out
Curry	36	b Lumpy	1	b Lumpy
Brett	6	not out	1	b May
Taylor	3	run out	0	b ditto
Byes	6	Byes	1	
	157		31	

KENT.

	1ſt inn.		2d inn.	
Duke of Dorſet	20	b Brett	10	c Francis
Bullen	1	c Francis	4	c Suter
Pattenden	7	c Aylward	72	b Brett
Wood	3	b Hogsfleſh	7	not out
Miller	8	b Nyren	7	c Aylward
Brazier	1	b Brett	31	b Brett
Booker	23	c Taylor	14	c Suter
White	25	b Hogsfleſh	26	c ditto
Lumpy	0	b Brett	6	c Curry
Simmons	11	c Francis	1	b Small
May	3	not out	3	b Nyren
Byes	2	Byes	13	
	104		194	

Kent won, by 110 runs.

LALEHAM BURWAY,
1775.

Hampſhire, (with the Duke of Dorſet) *againſt Surry* (with Miller & Minſhall.)

July 6.

HAMPSHIRE.

	1ſt inn.		2d inn.
Duke of Dorſet	0	b Wood	18
Brett	3	c Yalden	0
Nyren	12	c Lumpy	0
Small	4	c White	3
Lear	4	c Yalden	25
Suter	11	c ditto	11
Francis	4	b Wood	16
Aylward	1	c Edmeads	38
Taylor	7	b Lumpy	5
Barber	0	not out	3
Aborrow	4	c Wood	0
Byes	1	Byes	0
	51		119

SURRY.

	1ſt inn.		2d inn.	
Ld. Tankerville	0	b Brett	26	b Brett
Lumpy	9	b ditto	3	b ditto
White	0	b ditto	0	b ditto
Wood	12	not out	2	not out
Miller	0	c Taylor	42	c the Duke
Minſhall	8	c Small	45	b Barber
Palmer	15	b Brett	1	c Taylor
Quiddenden	11	b ditto	20	b Barber
T. Edmeads	13	c Small	2	c Brett
Yalden	2	b Brett	6	b ditto
Field	5	b ditto	15	run out
Byes	1	Byes	1	
	76		163	

Surry won by 69 runs.

SEVENOAKS, 1776.

Hampſhire, againſt all England.

June 26.

ALL ENGLAND.

	1ſt inn.		2d inn.	
Duke of Dorſet	6	b Brett	2	c Nyren
Lumpy	6	b Nyren	2	b Barber
Miller	4	c Small	6	c Suter
Bowra	1	b Brett	20	c Small
Bullen	29	c Francis	0	b Brett
Brazier	34	c Veck	19	not out
Pattenden	0	c Small	6	c Curry
Boreman	13	not out	9	c Francis
Booker	41	run out	6	c Taylor
White	23	hit wicket	0	c Suter
Wood	9	b Nyren	2	b Nyren
Byes	7	Byes	5	
	173		77	

HAMPSHIRE.

	1ſt inn.		2d inn.	
Aylward	6	c the Duke	3	b White
Small	45	c ditto	7	c Bullen
Lear	0	b Lumpy	1	c Bowra
Suter	5	c Booker	13	run out
Brett	3	c Bullen	1	not out
Curry	8	c Bowra	5	c Brazier
Francis	47	c Booker	9	b White
Taylor	42	c ditto	14	c Booker
Barber	4	not out	0	c Boreman
Nyren	70	c the Duke	19	c Bullen
Veck	0	c Bullen	10	b Lumpy
Byes	11	Byes	2	
	241		84	

Hampſhire won by 75 runs.

BROAD-HALFPENNY, 1776.

Hampshire, against all England.—returned Match.

July 4.

ALL ENGLAND.

	1st inn.		2d inn.	
Duke of Dorset	34	c Brett	1	b Francis
Lumpy	0	not out		
Miller	16	c Lear	12	c Suter
Bowra	31	b Francis	0	b Francis
Bullen	3	b Brett		
Brazier	36	b ditto	17	b Francis
Pattenden	20	b ditto	14	b ditto
Boreman	0	c Suter	39	not out
Booker	6	b Taylor	17	not out
White	4	b ditto	37	b Brett
Wood	4	b Barber		
Byes	9	Byes	0	
	163		137	

HAMPSHIRE.

	1st inn.		2d inn.	
Aylward	5	c Wood	19	b Lumpy
Small	12	c Bowra	56	b White
Lear	21	b Lumpy	23	b ditto
Suter	6	c Wood	18	c ditto
Brett	0	not out	0	not out
Curry	0	b Lumpy	7	b Wood
Francis	3	b ditto	13	b ditto
Taylor	20	c Bullen	22	b White
Nyren	6	b Lumpy	36	b Lumpy
Veck	14	c Brazier	14	b ditto
Barber	0	c Bullen	8	b White
Byes	0	Byes	6	
	87		222	

All England won, by 4 wickets.

SEVENOAKS, 1776.

Hampshire, against all England.

July 17.

ALL ENGLAND.

	1st inn.		2d inn.	
Duke of Dorset	9	c Aylward	0	b Francis
Lumpy	8	b Nyren	0	not out
Miller	27	c ditto	21	c Veck
Bowra	37	c Veck	8	b Francis
Bullen	4	b Brett	0	run out
Brazier	33	c Taylor	17	c Francis
Pattenden	8	c Small	3	b Brett
Boreman	5	not out	6	b ditto
Booker	1	c Small	2	c Taylor
White	9	c Lear	11	run out
Wood	7	b Nyren	0	c Lear
Byes	6	Byes	1	
	154		69	

HAMPSHIRE.

	1st inn.		2d inn.	
Aylward	13	c Bullen	0	c Boreman
Small	59	not out	2	c Wood
Lear	5	c Lumpy	47	not out
Suter	8	c ditto	13	c Wood
Brett	5	b Wood		
Curry	5	b Lumpy		
Francis	9	c Boreman	5	c Bowra
Taylor	8	b Wood		
Davis	1	b ditto		
Nyren	5	b Lumpy	22	not out
Veck	10	c ditto		
Byes	2	Byes	5	
	130		94	

Hampshire won by 6 wickets.

BROAD-HALFPENNY, 1776.

Hampshire, against all-England.

July 24.

ALL ENGLAND.

	1st inn.		2d inn.	
Duke of Dorset	5	b Brett	13	not out
Lumpy	16	not out		
Yalden	31	b Brett	15	b Brett
Bowra	36	c Francis		
Boyton	5	b Brett		
Brazier	6	b Francis	19	not out
Pattenden	1	c Suter	4	c Small
Boreman	0	b Brett	12	c Brett
Booker	2	c Taylor	0	c Barber
White	15	c Nyren	3	c Francis
Wood	3	c Small		
Byes	15	Byes	1	
	135		67	

HAMPSHIRE.

	1st inn.		2d inn.	
Aylward	13	b Lumpy	9	c Boreman
Small	20	b Wood	10	b Lumpy
Lear	0	c ditto	18	b ditto
Suter	2	run out	11	c White
Brett	0	c Booker	0	c Booker
Curry	6	c Wood	25	not out
Francis	12	b Lumpy	9	c Booker
Taylor	0	b ditto	5	c ditto
Veck	13	not out	8	c Yalden
Nyren	15	b White	12	b White
Barber	4	c Pattenden	3	c Yalden
Byes	3	Byes	3	
	88		113	

All England won by 5 wickets.

SEVENOAKS,
1777.
Hampſhire. againſt all England,
MAY 28, & 29.

ALL ENGLAND.

	1ſt inn.		2d inn.	
Duke of Dorſet	0	b Brett	5	c Taylor
Lumpy	1	b ditto	0	not out
Wood	1	b ditto	1	run out
White	8	c Veck	10	run out
Miller	27	c Suter	23	b Brett
Minſhall	60	not out	12	b Taylor
Bowra	2	b Brett	4	b ditto
Bullen	13	c Taylor	2	b Nyren
Booker	8	c Brett	2	b Brett
Yalden	6	c Suter	8	c Nyren
Pattenden	38	b Brett	0	c Suter
Byes	2	Byes	0	
	166		67	

HAMPSHIRE.

	1ſt inn.		2d inn.
Ld. Tankerville	3	b Wood	
Brett	9	not out	
Small	33	c White	
Francis	26	c Wood	
Nyren	37	b Lumpy	
Suter	46	b Wood	
Lear	7	b ditto	
Aylward	167	b Bullen	
Veck	16	b Lumpy	
Taylor	32	c Bullen	
Curry	22	c Minſhall	
Byes	5		
	403		

D

Hampſhire won by one innings & 170 runs.

LALEHAM BURWAY,
1777.

Hampshire, (with the Duke of Dorset (*against all Enlgand.*

AUGUST, 2,

HAMPSHIRE.

	1st inn.		2d inn.	
Duke of Dorset	37	b Lamborn	16	c Ld. Tankerv.
Small	28	c Edmeads	12	b Lumpy
Aylward	17	c ditto	0	c Ld. Tankerv.
Veck	2	b Lamborn	9	c Edmeads
Suter	7	c Yalden	23	b Wood
Taylor	0	not out	20	c Yalden
Lear	0	b Wood	70	b Wood
Nyren	10	b Lamborn	6	c Bullen
Francis	0	c Wood	5	run out
Curry	0	c Whitleshurst	22	b Lumpy
Brett	6	b Lumpy	0	not out
Byes	8	Byes	4	
	115		187	

ALL ENGLAND.

	1st inn.		2d inn.	
Ld. Tankerville	34	b the Duke	21	b Nyren
Edmeads	14	c Suter	5	b Brett
Yalden	1	c Veck	29	not out
Lumpy	7	not out	3	b Brett
Minshall	7	*hurt his knee*		
Field (v Minsh.)	16	run out	0	b Brett
Wood	5	b Brett	4	run out
Miller	0	c Francis	2	c Francis
Bowra	28	b Brett	8	b Nyren
Bullen	3	b ditto	38	c Curry
Lamborn	0	b ditto	3	b Brett
Whitleshurst	24	b the Duke	6	c Small
Byes	4	Byes	1	
	143		120	

Hampshire won by 39 runs.

BROAD-HALFPENNY, 1777.

Hampshire, against all England.

AUGUST 9, 10, & 11.

ALL ENGLAND.

	1st inn.		2d. inn.	
Yalden	1	b Brett	44	c Taylor
Wood	9	b Francis	0	b Small
Miller	4	b ditto	65	b Brett
Minshall	21	b Brett	16	b ditto
Bowra	2	run out	6	b Francis
Bullen	1	b Brett	27	c Suter
Duke of Dorset	2	c Ld. Tankerville	0	b Small
Clifford	7	b Brett	4	run out
White	3	b Nyren	3	b Small
Booker	5	b ditto	29	c Nyren
Lumpy	1	not out	5	not out
Byes	4	Byes	8	
	60		207	

HAMPSHIRE.

	1st inn.		2d inn.	
Aylward	15	c Miller	0	b Wood
Veck	54	b White	0	not out
Small	3	b Wood	8	run out
Suter	22	c Wood	1	c Yalden
Lear	11	c Yalden	0	c ditto
Ld. Tankerville	0	run out	7	c Miller
Taylor	0	b Lumpy	2	b Lumpy
Nyren	18	b White	17	c Yalden
Curry	22	b Lumpy	2	run out
Francis	46	b the Duke	6	b Lumpy
Brett	6	not out	1	c Bullen
Byes	0	Byes	1	
	197		45	

All England won by 25 runs. Seven to four at starting, and at one part of the game 8 to 1 in favor of Hampshire.

GUILDFORD,
1777.

Hampshire, against all England.

AUGUST 20.

ALL ENGLAND.

	1st inn.		2d inn.	
Ld. Tankerville	1	b Brett	46	b Nyren
Edmeads	1	b ditto	6	c Francis
Minshall	33	not out	0	b Mann
Lamborn	0	b Nyren	10	c Aylward
Lumpy	1	run out	6	not out
Bullen	0	b Nyren	20	b Mann
Miller	2	run out	64	b ditto
Bowra	5	b Nyren	12	run out
Wood	0	b Brett	17	thrown out by Brett
Yalden	6	c Taylor	42	b Nyren
Phillips	0	b Nyren	20	c Veck
Byes	1	Byes	7	
	50		250	

HAMPSHIRE.

	1st inn.		2d. inn.	
Nyren	4	b Lumpy	5	not out
Suter	14	b Wood	9	not out
Small	15	c Minshall	36	c Wood
Aylward	30	c Bowra	0	b Lumpy
Veck	1	c Yalden	17	c Bullen
Francis	15	c Ld. Tankerv.	9	b Lamborn
Curry	3	b Lumpy	9	b Lumpy
N. Mann	27	c Bullen	14	c Edmeads
Taylor	19	c Edmeads	58	c Wood
Barber	0	b Lumpy	0	b Lumpy
Brett	3	not out	3	b Bullen
Byes	2	Byes	8	
	133		168	

Hampshire won by 1 wicket.

GUILDFORD, 1777.

Hampshire, against all England.

ALL-ENGLAND.	1st inn.	2d inn.	HAMPSHIRE.	1st inn.	2d inn
Ld. Tankerville	1	45	Francis	15	9
Miller	3	65	Aylward	30	0
Yalden	6	42	Small	14	35
Bullen	0	20	Mann	24	11
C. Phillips	0	20	Taylor	20	60
Bowra	3	12	Suter	10	5
Minshall	33	0	Nyren	5	5
Edmeads	1	7	Veck	1	16
Lumpy	1	2	Curry	6	8
Wood	0	7	Brett	3	4
Lamborn	0	9	Barber	0	0
Byes	2	5	Byes	5	0
	50	234		133	153

CHERTSEY, 1777.

Hampshire, against all England.—returned Match.

HAMPSHIRE.	1st inn.	2d inn.	ALL-ENGLAND.	1st inn.	2d inn.
Veck	2	9	Bullen	3	36
Curry	0	22	Minshall	7	3
Small	28	12	Miller	0	2
Aylward	17	0	L. Tankerv.	34	21
Suter	8	23	Yalden	1	29
Lear	0	72	Bowra	29	8
Duke of Dorset	37	14	White	40	12
Francis	0	5	Edmeads	12	5
Nyren	10	6	Lumpy	6	3
Taylor	0	20	Wood	6	0
Brett	6	0	Lambert	0	8
Byes	7	4	Byes	5	1
	115	187		143	128

Hampshire won, by 31 runs.

SEVENOAKS, 1778.

Hampshire, against all England.

JUNE 29.

ALL ENGLAND.

	1st inn.		2d inn.	
Clifford	10	b Francis	15	b Nyren
Lumpy	11	b Mann	4	b Brett
Miller	0	run out	33	b ditto
Minshall	0	c Taylor	12	c Suter
Bowra	14	run out	2	b Nyren
White	13	b Brett	11	b Mann
Wood	7	b Francis	7	not out
Yalden	19	c Taylor	22	run out
Lamborn	2	not out	4	c Veck
Bullen	5	b Brett	6	c Curry
Booker	0	b Mann	4	b Mann
Byes	7	Byes	2	
	88		122	

HAMPSHIRE.

	1st inn.		2d inn.	
Small	1	c Yalden	6	b Lamborn
Suter	3	b Lumpy	2	not out
Lear	4	c Yalden		
Nyren	3	b Lumpy	38	c Yalden
Francis	24	b Lamborn	0	c Lumpy
Veck	2	c Wood	53	not out
Taylor	0	c Minshall	5	c Wood
Curry	1	not not	0	b Lamborn
Brett	0	c Wood		
Bedster	12	c Minshall	7	c Yalden
N. Mann	16	b Lumpy	19	c Bowra
Byes	5	Byes	10	
	71		140	

Hampshire won by 3 wickets.

BROAD-HALFPENNY, 1779.

Hampshire, against all England.

JULY 7.

ALL ENGLAND.

	1st inn.		2d inn.	
Bullen	0	b Nyren	12	not out
Bedster	3	b Francis	34	b Brett
Miller	1	c Suter	9	b Nyren
Minshall	31	b Taylor	0	run out
White	33	b ditto	16	b Nyren
Bowra	2	run out	29	run out
Yalden	24	not out	10	c Taylor
Booker	2	b Taylor	3	c Francis
Lumpy	19	c ditto	11	b Nyren
Wood	26	b Mann	0	c Suter
Lamborn	0	b ditto	1	b Nyren
Byes	2	Byes	5	
	143		130	

HAMPSHIRE.

	1st inn.		2d inn.	
Aburrow	14	b Lamborn	0	b Lamborn
Francis	0	b ditto	23	b Lumpy
Suter	22	c ditto	17	not out
Veck	7	c Wood	7	c Lumpy
Small	49	not out	4	b ditto
Taylor	1	b Lamborn	5	b Lamborn
N. Mann	7	c Yalden	0	b ditto
Lear	17	b Lumpy	2	c Yalden
Nyren	5	c Miller	3	b Lumpy
Stone	0	run out	0	run out
Brett	19	c Bullen	12	b Wood
Byes	11	Byes	3	
	152		76	

All England won by, 45 runs.

LALEHAM BURWAY,
1778.

Surry (with Miller) *againſt Hampſhire.*

OCTOBER 6.

SURRY.

	1ſt inn.		2d inn.	
Edmeads	1	run out	12	c Francis
Yalden	24	c Small	14	b Brett
Minſhall	75	b Brett	17	b Mann
Lumpy	0	b ditto	4	not out
Lamborn	0	b ditto	0	c Lear
Field	18	b Mann	0	b Brett
Bedſter	48	b Taylor	19	b Nyren
Muggeridge	4	c ditto	3	b Mann
White	23	not out	1	c Steward
Mills	1	run out	10	b Mann
Miller	42	b Taylor	20	c Nyren
Byes	2	Byes	5	
	238		105	

HAMPSHIRE.

	1ſt inn.		2d inn.	
H. Bonham, Eſq.	4	b Lumpy	9	ſtumpt Yalden
Small	6	b ditto	3	run out
Nyren	9	b Lamborn	0	c Wood
N. Mann	2	b ditto	4	b Lumpy
Brett	6	c Muggeridge	0	c Minſhall
Curry	0	c Yalden	10	b Lumpy
Steward	3	b Lamborn	0	not out
Taylor	18	not out	5	b Lamborn
Francis	15	b Lamborn	11	b Lumpy
Lear	31	b ditto	17	c Edmeads
Suter	17	b ditto	20	b Lumpy
Byes	5	Byes	10	
	116		89	

Surry won, by 140 runs.

STOKE-DOWN,

1779.

Hampſhire, againſt all England.

JUNE 13 & 14.

ALL ENGLAND.

	1ſt inn.		2d inn.	
Bullen	5	run out	4	c Suter
Bedſter	23	c Small	26	b Mann
Miller	23	b Nyren	25	c Suter
Minſhall	7	c Small	17	c Small
Rimmington	2	b Nyren	19	b Nyren
Bowra	9	c Aylward	9	c Ld. Tankerville
Mills	5	b Nyren	34	b Nyren
Clifford	3	b ditto	34	c Ld. Tankerville
Booker	1	not out	7	c Curry
Lumpy	0	run out	4	not out
Lamborn	0	b Francis	0	c Nyren
Byes	2	Byes	1	
	80		180	

HAMPSHIRE.

	1ſt inn.		2d inn.	
Ld. Tankerville	6	c Booker	12	b Lamborn
Small	16	b Lumpy	11	b Lumpy
Aylward	12	b Lamborn	27	b ditto
Veck	30	b Lumpy	39	not out
Suter	44	b ditto		
Taylor	9	b ditto		
Lear	2	c Bullen		
Curry	11	b Lamborn	25	not out
Francis	0	c Bowra		
Mann	4	b Lamborn		
Nyren	0	not out	6	b Bullen
Byes	2	Byes	5	
	136		125	

Hampſhire won by 6 wickets.

SEVENOAKS,
1779.

Hampſhire, againſt all England.

JUNE 23, 24, 25, & 26.

ALL-ENGLAND.

	1ſt inn.		2d inn.	
Bedſter	22	c Small	37	b Francis
Mills	3	b Mann	7	c Suter
Miller	0	hit wicket	0	b Mann
Bullen	1	b Mann	5	not out
Minſhall	3	b Nyren	4	run out
Bowra	0	b ditto	11	c Mann
Yalden	0	b ditto	2	c ditto
Clifford	2	b Mann	12	c Veck
White	3	c Taylor	6	b Nyren
Lamborn	1	c Mann	0	b Mann
Lumpy	21	not out	3	b ditto
Byes	0	Byes	0	
	56		87	

HAMPSHIRE.

	1ſt inn.		2d inn.
Curry	16	b Bullen	
Aylward	13	b ditto	
Small	3	b Lambert	
Ld. Tankerville	6	b Lumpy	
Veck	79	b Lamborn	
Mann	56	b ditto	
Francis	1	b ditto	
Taylor	13	b ditto	
Suter	11	c Bowra	
Lear	9	c Yalden	
Nyren	14	not out	
Byes	11		
	232		

Hampſhire won, by one innings and 89 runs.

LALEHAM BURWAY, 1779.

Surry against Kent, (two men given each side)

AUGUST 9, & 10.

SURRY.

	1st inn.		2d inn.	
Ld. Tankerville	11	c Bowra	16	c Bowra
Bedster	0	b Bullen	20	c Boreman
Lamborn	0	b Boreman	3	b Bullen
Minshall	40	run out	11	c Miller
Simmons	2	b May	2	b Bullen
Edmead	20	c Booker	3	c Pattenden
Yalden	27	c Rimmington	2	b Bullen
Berwick	1	b Boreman	9	not out
Mills	11	c Bowra	8	c Aylward
Field	7	b Boreman	27	c Bullen
Lumpy	4	not out	3	b May
Byes	0	Byes	4	
	123		108	

KENT.

	1st inn.		2d inn.	
Boreman	0	b Lamborn		
Veck	55	c Yalden	9	b Lumpy
Aylward	4	c ditto	11	c Yalden
Bullen	17	b Lamborn	20	not out
Booker	1	b Lumpy		
Bowra	15	c Lamborn	10	not out
Clifford	1	b Lumpy		
Miller	25	b ditto	25	b Lamborn
Rimmington	15	b Lamborn	6	c Yalden
Pattenden	4	c Bedster	7	b Lamborn
May	2	not out		
Byes	2	Byes	3	
	141		91	

Kent won, by 5 wickets.

BROAD-HALFPENNY,
1779.

Hampshire, against all England.

AUGUST 23.

HAMPSHIRE.

	1st inn.		2d inn.	
Curry	2		9	b Lamborn
Mann	45		23	b ditto
Small	66		6	b Lumpy
Veck	8		14	b Bullen
Suter	10		24	c ditto
Lear	2		58	c Yalden
Taylor	6		2	b Lamborn
Berwick	0		10	not out
Stewart	4		2	b Lumpy
Nyren	1		14	c Aylward
Bowra	16		12	b Lamborn
Byes	7	Byes	8	
	167		182	

ALL ENGLAND.

	1st inn.		2d inn.	
Bedster	8		2	b Nyren
Ld. Tankerville	0		12	c ditto
Yalden	10		0	b Berwick
Field	17		16	c Veck
Miller	0		37	b Mann
Minshall	0		4	b Nyren
Lamborn	0		0	b Mann
Bullen	3		6	b ditto
Lumpy	4		1	not out
Clifford	17		3	c Curry
Aylward	51		3	b Nyren
Byes	2	Byes	4	
	112		88	

Hampshire won, by 149 runs.

CHERTSEY,

1779.

Kent, (with two of Hampſhire) *againſt Surry*.

AUGUST, 30,

KENT.

	1ſt inn.		2d inn.	
Clifford	1	b Lumpy		
Veck	55	c Yalden	9	b Lumpy
Boreman	0	b Lamborn		
Bullen	17	b ditto	5	not out
Rimmington	15	c Yalden	5	c Yalden
Pattenden	4	c Bedſter	8	b Lamborn
Booker	1	b Lumpy		
Miller	24	b ditto	26	b Lamborn
Bowra	15	c Lamborn	12	not out
Aylward	15	not out	16	b Lamborn
May	8	run out		
Byes	0	Byes	0	
	155		81	

SURRY.

	1ſt inn.		2d inn.	
Ld. Tankerville	11	c Bowra	16	c Bowra
Edmeads	20	c Booker	3	c Pattenden
Bedſter	0	b Bullen	20	c Boreman
Minſhall	40	run out	11	c Miller
Simmons	2	b May	2	b Bullen
Yalden	27	c Rimmington	3	b ditto
Field	7	b Boreman	26	not out
Lumpy	4	not out	3	b May
Mills	11	c Bowra	8	c Aylward
Lamborn	0	b Boreman	3	b Bullen
Berwick	10	b Bullen	8	b ditto
Byes	0	Byes	0	
	132		103	

Kent won, by 5 wickets.

MOULSEY-HURST,
1779.

Hants. (with Berwick&Bowra) *ag. all England*, (with Aylward)

SEPTEMBER 13, 14, 15, 16.

HAMPSHIRE.

	1ſt inn.		2d inn.	
Lear	21	c Bullen	10	
Taylor	80	c Bedſter	3	
Mann	38	b ditto	1	
Small	5	c Yalden	9	
Veck	3	c Bedſter	43	
Suter	5	b Bullen	11	not out
Bowra	5	b Lumpy	6	
Curry	0	run out	35	
Nyren	2	b Lumpy	23	not out
Berwick	1	b ditto	19	
Stewart	6	run out		
Byes	6	Byes	2	
	172		162	

ALL ENGLAND.

	1ſt inn.		2d inn.	
Bedſter	1	b Nyren	7	
Field	9	b ditto	46	
Aylward	4	c Bowra	6	
Miller	7	b Mann	34	
Minſhall	0	b Berwick	34	
Bullen	35	c Taylor	12	
Clifford	33	c ditto	21	
Yalden	0	c Berwick	25	
Edmeads	0	c Veck	0	
Lumpy	2	b Nyren	52	
Lamborn	0	not not	3	
Byes	0	Byes	2	not out
	91		242	

Hampſhire won by 2 wickets,

SEVENOAKS,
1780.
A SELECT MATCH.
JUNE 27, 28.

DUKE OF DORSET.

	1ſt inn.		2b inn.	
Duke of Dorſet	0		6	b Berwick
Ld. Tankerville	4		1	c Yalden
Minſhall	13		5	b Berwick
Bedſter	8		11	c Aylward
Booker	0		7	c Aylward
Bowra	33		4	b Gibſon
Bullen	8		34	b Berwick
Field	1		13	not out
Pattenden	9		0	c Aylward
Boreman	13		6	c Stone
Lumpy	2		0	c Berwick
Byes	2	Byes	5	
	93		92	

SIR HORACE MANN.

	1ſt inn.		2d inn.	
Stone	9	c Lumpy		
Yalden	0	b Bullen	15	c Bedſter
Berwick	1	b Lumpy	10	b Bullen
Miller	13	b ditto	24	not out
Aylward	47	b ditto	12	not out
May	4	run out		
Clifford	8	b Bullen	20	b Lumpy
Mills	4	b ditto		
Hoſmer	6	b ditto		
Rimmington	11	run out		
Gibſon	0	not out		
Byes	2	Byes	0	
	105		81	

Sir Horace Mann won, by 7 wickets.

BOURNE PADDOCK,
1780.
SELECT MATCH,—returned.
AUGUST 21, 22, 23.

DUKE OF DORSET.

	1ſt inn.		2d inn.	
Stanford	9	b Gibſon	10	c Miller
Bullen	0	b Clifford	30	c Clifford
Bedſter	23	b ditto	24	b Gibſon
Ld. Tankerville	30	c Yalden	9	c Hoſmer
Booker	2	b Clifford	16	not out
Bowra	0	b Gibſon	2	c Yalden
W. Pattenden	15	b ditto	32	b Clifford
T. Pattenden	0	b Clifford	7	c Aylward
Boreman	6	b Gibſon	4	b Gibſon
Lumpy	10	not out	25	c ditto
Newman	2	b Gibſon	0	b Clifford
Byes	0	Byes	4	
	97		163	

SIR HORACE MANN.

	1ſt inn.		2d. inn.	
Stone	4	b Lumpy	8	b Bullen
T. Rimmington	17	b Boreman	9	b Lumpy
B. Rimmington	62	b Lumpy	15	b Bedſter
Aylward	4	run out	17	c ditto
Miller	3	c Bullen	5	b ditto
Hoſmer	36	c Booker	3	b Lumpy
Clifford	1	c Bullen	2	c Bowra
Mills	8	run out	5	b Bedſter
Yalden	9	not out	22	not out
Gibſon	1	c Newman	8	c Lumpy
May	0	run out	0	c Bedſter
Byes	4	Byes	3	
	149		97	

The Duke of Dorſet won, by 14 runs.

BOURNE PADDOCK,
1780.

Hampſhire, againſt Kent,—with *Surry* divided.

AUGUST 30, and two following days.

KENT.

	1ſt inn.		2d inn.	
T. Rimmington	25	b Nyren	7	run out
Bedſter	12	b Mann	8	b Lamborn
Bullen	7	c Ld. Tankerville	12	c Small
Aylward	9	b Nyren	24	b Nyren
B. Rimmington	4	b Lamborn	4	c Small
Miller	7	c Small	37	b Curry
Bowra	31	b Veck	1	c Mann
Yalden	52	c Freemantle	34	b Lamborn
Clifford	25	b Nyren	7	c Taylor
Lumpy	6	c Suter	4	not out
Berwick	6	not out	5	b Freemantle
Byes	13	Byes	1	
	197		144	

HAMPSHIRE.

	1ſt inn.		2d inn.	
Curry	0	c Bullen	36	b Lumpy
Field	13	b Clifford	0	run out
Mann	6	b Lumpy	33	b Clifford
Taylor	2	b Clifford	0	c T. Rimmington
Small	22	c Lumpy	19	b Lumpy
Nyren	4	c Bullen	0	c Bowra
Veck	7	c Aylward	2	b Clifford
Lamborn	2	b Clifford	3	not out
Suter	14	c Berwick	0	b Clifford
Ld. Tankerville	4	b Clifford	1	c Aylward
Freemantle	1	not out	0	c ditto
Byes	5	Byes	2	
	80	*F*	96	

Kent won, by 166 runs. In this match Yalden got 12 runs in two following ſtrokes; Bedſter 7; and Lumpy 6.

STOKE DOWN,

1780.

Kent, againſt Hampſhire—with *Surry* divided.

SEPTEMBER 20, 21, 22.

HAMPSHIRE.

	1ſt inn.		2d inn.	
Small	0	c Yalden	6	b Lumpy
Ld. Tankerville	3	b Clifford	2	c Aylward
Veck	16	b Lumpy	23	c Bullen
Mann	30	c Clifford	10	b Lumpy
Curry	42	run out	1	run out
Nyren	11	b Lumpy	4	not out
Taylor	17	c ditto	2	b Lumpy
Suter	36	b ditto	6	b Clifford
Freemantle	4	b Clifford	0	b Lumpy
Wood	5	b Lumpy	1	b ditto
Lamborn	0	not out	4	b ditto
Byes	5	Byes	1	
	169		60	

KENT.

	1ſt inn.		2d inn.	
B. Rimmington	7	b Lamborn	38	b Nyren
Bullen	0	b ditto	15	b Freemantle
Miller	50	c Mann	3	c Small
Aylward	26	c Nyren	3	b Nyren
T. Rimmington	0	c Mann	3	b Lamborn
Bedſter	24	c ditto	10	c Nyren
Yalden	0	b Lamborn	4	b ditto
Berwick	2	b Wood	4	not out
Bowra	3	c Freemantle	1	run out
Clifford	33	not out	12	b Nyren
Lumpy	31	b Lamborn	4	b ditto
Byes	3	Byes	4	
	179		101	

Kent won, by 51 runs

BOURN PADDOCK, 1780.

SEPTEMBER 2,——*A Single Innings.*

HAMPSHIRE.

Lumpy	1	b Bullen
Suter	5	c Clifford
Small	4	b Bullen
Veck	8	c Aylward
N. Mann	5	b Bedſter
	23	

KENT.

Miller	0	b Lumpy
Bedſter	3	b Mann
Aylward	0	c Veck
Clifford	3	b Lumpy
Bullen	16	c Small
	22	

MOULSEY-HURST, 1781.

Hampſhire, againſt all England.

ALL ENGLAND.

	1ſt inn.	2d inn.
Bullen	15 c Mann	4 c Mann
Clifford	15 c ditto	14 c ditto
Aylward	0 b Lumpy	7 b Lumpy
Miller	0 b ditto	1 c Small
Bedſter	0 b ditto	14 c Mann
	30	40

HAMPSHIRE.

	1ſt inn.	2d inn.
Small	15 b Bullen	4 c Aylward
Veck	10 c ditto	13 b ditto
Suter	10 b ditto	20 b ditto
Lumpy	1 b ditto	8 b Bullen
Mann	0 b ditto	67 b Aylward
	36	112

STOKE-DOWN, 1781.

Hampshire, against all England.

JUNE 6, 7, 8, 9.

ALL-ENGLAND.

	1st inn.		2d inn.	
Miller	16	b Mann	14	c Taylor
T. Rimmington	0	b Lamborn	4	b Mann
Aylward	25	b ditto	73	c Bedster
M. Rimmington	2	b ditto	16	not out
Bullen	16	b Mann	1	b Mann
Clifford	22	b Lamborn	48	b Lamborn
B. Rimmington	1	b ditto	31	b Nyren
Bowra	13	not out	8	b Mann
Yalden	0	b Mann	7	b Nyren
Boreman	1	b Lamborn	17	b Freemantle
Lumpy	1	b ditto	12	b Mann
Byes	4	Byes	1	
	101		232	

HAMPSHIRE.

	1st inn.		2d inn.	
Bedster	5	c Yalden	49	b Bowra
Mann	10	b Clifford	73	b Lumpy
Taylor	12	c Yalden	1	not out
Freemantle	19	not out	5	not out
Curry	11	c Clifford		
Small	47	b Lumpy		
Veck	12	c B. Rimmington		
Suter	66	c M. Rimmington		
Lear	15	c Bullen		
Nyren	8	b Lumpy		
Lamborn	0	c Clifford		
Byes	1			
	206		128	

Hampshire won by 8 wickets.

SEVENOAKS, 1781.

East Kent, against West Kent,—two of *Hants.* on each side.

JUNE 20, 21.

EAST-KENT.

	1st inn.		2d inn.	
Miller	29	c Suter	0	b Lumpy
Clifford	32	b Lumpy	5	b Bullen
Small	5	c Suter	3	c Suter
Hosmer	9	b Lumpy	37	not out
Veck	5	c Suter	5	c Wood
B. Rimmington	23	c ditto	1	c Bowra
Pemmell	0	c Lumpy	7	b Bedster
W. Pattenden	12	b Bedster	6	c Suter
T. Rimmington	11	c Lumpy	9	c Lumpy
Holness	9	b Bedster	0	c Bullen
Lamborn	1	not out	6	c Mann
Byes	0	Byes	5	
	136		84	

WEST-KENT.

	1st inn.		2d inn.	
Bedster	1	c Veck		
Mann	21	b Clifford	37	not out
Suter	34	b Lamborn		
Wood	2	b Clifford		
Bullen	7	b Lamborn	26	not out
Bowra	18	c Pemmell		
T. Pattenden	50	not out		
Stanford	6	b Clifford		
Webb	17	c Hosmer		
Mills	0	b Clifford		
Lumpy	0	b Lamborn		
Byes	2	Byes	0	
	158		63	

West-Kent won, by 10 wickets.

BOURNE PADDOCK,

1781.

Kent, (with Lumpy and Yalden) *against all England.*

JULY 18, 19, 20.

ALL ENGLAND.

	1ſt inn.		2d inn.	
Bedſter	0	b Lumpy	3	c Clifford
Curry	5	b ditto	5	c Yalden
Taylor	6	b Clifford	3	b Lumpy
Veck	2	c Yalden	26	c ditto
Small	7	c Clifford	17	c Yalden
Suter	3	c ditto	14	run out
Mann	2	c Bullen	7	c Yalden
Nyren	5	b Clifford	22	b Lumpy
Freemantle	1	c ditto	6	b ditto
Lamborn	8	c ditto	0	not out
Lear	14	not out	53	b Lumpy
Byes	6	Byes	2	
	59		158	

KENT.

	1ſt inn.		2d inn.	
Bullen	4	c Suter	13	b Nyren
Clifford	26	b Nyren	57	b Freemantle
Aylward	29	c Veck	25	c Suter
Webb	18	b Lamborn	2	c Taylor
Bowra	15	b ditto	10	b Freemantle
Rimmington	11	b ditto	20	c Suter
Pattenden	15	c Taylor	16	c Taylor
Hogben	13	b Nyren	15	c Curry
Yalden	18	not out	0	b Mann
Lumpy	7	b Freemantle	10	not out
Miller	29	c Nyren	14	run out
Byes	6	Byes	4	
	181		186	

Kent won, by 150 runs.

BROAD-HALFPENNY,

1781.

Hamſhire, (with Lamborn) *againſt Kent*, (with Bedſter)

JULY 30, and two following days.

KENT.

	1ſt inn.		2d inn.	
Bullen	5	b Purchaſe	54	run out
Clifford	66	b Nyren	13	c Suter
Aylward	6	b Purchaſe	28	b Veck
Bedſter	10	run out	1	c Suter
Bowra	29	b Purchaſe	42	not out
Miller	45	b Nyren	10	run out
Rimmington	21	b ditto	15	c Nyren
Pattenden	0	b ditto	2	c Veck
Hogben	12	b Lamborn	3	run out
Boreman	5	not out	17	c Veck
Webb	2	b Lamborn	0	b Nyren
Byes	17	Byes	3	
	218		188	

HAMPSHIRE.

	1ſt inn.		2d inn.	
Lear	17	c Webb	10	c Clifford
Mann	49	b Bullen	41	not out
Curry	3	b ditto	10	c Clifford
Suter	21	run out	0	b Bullen
Small	0	b Bullen	34	c Bowra
Veck	26	c Bowra	44	b Clifford
Nyren	5	b Bullen	3	c Bowra
Taylor	34	b ditto	23	c Aylward
Purchaſe	5	not out	3	c Bowra
Freemantle	11	b Bullen	5	b Clifford
Lamborn	4	c ditto	0	c Aylward
Byes	10	Byes	10	
	185		183	

Kent won, by 38 runs.

BOURNE PADDOCK, 1781.

A SELECT MATCH.

AUGUST 8, 9, 10, 11.

DUKE OF DORSET.

	1st inn.		2d inn.	
Suter	58	c Hogben	56	b Lamborn
Bedster	19	c Aylward	20	c Small
Ld. Tankerville	11	c Hogben	9	b Clifford
Bowra	5	b Clifford	3	b ditto
Bullen	10	c Martin	36	run out
Pattenden	26	not out	6	b Clifford
Yalden	19	c Pattenden	5	b Lamborn
Stanford	4	b Lamborn	11	not out
Boreman	0	b Clifford	3	b Lamborn
Mann	4	b ditto	21	c Pattenden
Lumpy	12	b Lamborn	13	c Hogben
Byes	2	Byes	1	
	170		184	

SIR HORACE MANN.

	1st inn.		2d. inn.	
Small	21	b Lumpy	28	c Yalden
Aylward	36	b Boreman	44	b Lumpy
Clifford	24	b Lumpy	3	c Bullen
Miller	31	c Stanford	3	b ditto
Hodges	7	b Bullen	1	run out
Rimmington	3	c ditto	3	c Bedster
Pattenden	13	b Lumpy	3	b Lumpy
Hogben	1	b ditto	15	b ditto
Martin	2	c ditto	0	not out
Lamborn	2	not out	0	b Lumpy
Webb	3	c Lumpy	0	run out
Byes	4	Byes	1	
	147		101	

Duke of Dorset won, by 106 runs.

BOURNE PADDOCK,
1781.

Hampſhire, (with Lamborn) *againſt Kent*, (with Bedſter)

AUGUST 27, 28.

HAMPSHIRE.

	1ſt inn.		2d inn.	
Lear	2	c Hogben	11	run out
Mann	16	c Bullen	17	b Bowra
Veck	2	b ditto	14	c Aylward
Small	5	run out	14	c Clifford
Suter	16	c Boreman	13	c Sim. v Boreman
Nyren	7	b Clifford	1	not out
Freemantle	3	c Aylward	8	b Clifford
Purchaſe	0	b Clifford	24	b Bullen
Curry	4	c Bullen	3	b Bowra
Skinner	3	not out	0	b Clifford
Lamborn	2	b Clifford	0	c Aylward
Byes	0	Byes	1	
	60		106	

KENT.

	1ſt inn.		2d inn.	
Webb	0	b Lamborn	4	run out
Clifford	5	b ditto	4	b Lamborn
Rimmington	7	run out	0	b Purchaſe
Bullen	0	b Lamborn	21	c Mann
Bedſter	3	c Purchaſe	8	not out
Miller	3	c Lear	1	b Nyren
Bowra	17	b Nyren	2	b ditto
Aylward	32	c Lear	21	c Lear
Hogben	13	b Lamborn	5	b Lamborn
Pattenden	5	b Nyren	4	b Nyren
Boreman	0	not out	0	c Veck
Byes	3	Byes	0	
	88		70	

G

Hampſhire won by 8 runs.

SEVENOAKS,
1782.

Kent, (with Lumpy & Bedster,) *against all Enlgand.*

JULY 3, 4, 5.

KENT.

	1st inn.		2d inn.	
Bullen	5	c Francis	11	not out
Clifford	0	c Taylor	15	b Mann
Aylward	3	c Francis	17	run out
Bedster	25	c Curry	12	c Curry
Bowra	4	b Harris	48	c Lear
Brazier	1	b ditto	0	c Field
Pattenden	7	b Mann		
Hosmer	6	c Hall	20	not out
Booker	29	not out		
Ring	3	c Small	2	b Mann
Lumpy	17	b Curry		
Byes	2	Byes	2	
	102		127	

HAMPSHIRE.

	1st inn.		2d inn.	
Small	2	c Booker	15	c Bowra
Veck	7	c Bullen	0	c Aylward
Mann	6	b Lumpy	13	c Bullen
Curry	8	c Clifford	6	b Clifford
Field	16	not out	6	b ditto
Lear	1	c Bowra	25	c Hosmer
Taylor	0	c Booker	6	c Booker
Hall	4	b Clifford	2	not out
Francis	10	b Lumpy	15	b Lumpy
Harris	27	c Aylward	1	c Bullen
Suter	5	c Bullen	48	b Clifford
Byes	1	Byes	3	
	87		140	

Kent won, by 4 wickets.

STOKE DOWNS,
1782.

Kent, (with Lumpy and Bedſter) *againſt Hampſhire.*

JULY 11, 12, 13, 15.

KENT.

	1ſt inn.		2d inn.	
Bullen	5	b Harris	1	b Harris
Clifford	0	b Freemantle	8	b Purchaſe
Aylward	75	b ditto	0	c Harris
Bedſter	63	b ditto	0	c ditto
Bowra	51	c Purchaſe	21	b Purchaſe
Brazier	37	b Freemantle	9	c Taylor
Miller	0	b ditto	7	c Small
Hogben	12	c Small	9	not out
Booker	0	c Veck	8	run out
Ring	10	run out	4	b Purchaſe
Lumpy	2	not out	5	c Harris
Byes	2	Byes	0	
	257		72	

HAMPSHIRE.

	1ſt inn.		2d inn.	
Suter	21	c Ring	12	b Clifford
Curry	5	b Clifford	7	b Lumpy
Small	0	b Lumpy	8	b ditto
Lear	6	c Booker	8	b Clifford
Mann	34	b Clifford	8	b Lumpy
Veck	18	c Bedſter	12	b Clifford
Taylor	4	b Lumpy	4	b ditto
Purchaſe	17	c Bedſter	3	c ditto
Francis	3	run out	0	run out
Freemantle	4	c Bullen	2	not out
Harris	6	not out	2	b Lumpy
Byes	3	Byes	0	
	121		66	

Kent won, by 142 runs.

BOURN PADDOCK,
1782.

Hampſhire, (with Lumpy) *againſt all England.*

JULY 25, 26.

HAMPSHIRE.

	1ſt inn.		2d inn.	
Nyren	0	b Clifford	13	b Bullen
Mann	5	b Bullen	21	b Clifford
Suter	2	b Clifford	6	c ditto
Small	15	b Francis	3	c Bullen
Purchaſe	33	b Clifford	2	c Clifford
Veck	12	b ditto	4	c Aylward
Curry	0	b ditto	32	b Bullen
Taylor	0	b ditto	2	c Aylward
Harris	1	b ditto	4	run out
Lumpy	3	b Bullen	6	not out
Lear	15	not out	23	b Bedſter
Byes	2	Byes	12	
	88		128	

ALL ENGLAND.

	1ſt inn.		2d inn.	
Francis	17	b Lumpy	1	b Lumpy
Bedſter	0	c Suter	0	c Nyren
Bullen	11	c Nyren	2	b ditto
Brazier	26	b Lumpy	23	run out
Aylward	0	b ditto	4	c Veck
Bowra	6	c Veck	0	b Nyren
Hogben	1	c Taylor	0	b ditto
Ring	3	b Nyren	7	c Taylor
Pattenden	1	b Lumpy	7	not out
Clifford	28	c Taylor	46	c Veck
Booker	11	not out	6	b Nyren
Byes	4	Byes	3	
	108		99	

Hampſhire won by 9 runs.

BROAD-HALFPENNY,
1782.

Hampſhire, (with Lumpy) *againſt all England*, returned match,

AUGUST 8, 9, 10.

HAMPSHIRE.

	1ſt inn.		2d inn.	
Mann	2	b Bullen	44	run out
Purchaſe	3	b Clifford	23	c Bedſter
Lear	2	c Bullen	6	b Clifford
Suter	14	c Yalden	0	b Bullen
Small	0	c Bowra	8	c Yalden
Veck	4	b Bullen	3	b Clifford
Curry	21	not out	0	run out
Nyren	3	b Clifford	1	b Bullen
Taylor	9	c Aylward	0	b Clifford
Lumpy	4	b Bullen	2	c Francis
Harris	0	b Clifford	2	not out
Byes	2	Byes	4	
	64		93	

ALL ENGLAND.

	1ſt inn.		2d inn.	
Miller	1	b Nyren	25	c Harris
Bowra	0	run out	15	c Lumpy
Clifford	1	c Purchaſe	31	b ditto
Ring	10	c Small	9	b ditto
Yalden	24	not out	16	b Nyren
Aylward	19	c Suter	18	ſtumpt out
Bedſter	11	c Suter	0	b Nyren
Francis	21	b Lumpy	4	c Small
Brazier	2	b ditto	39	b Lumpy
Bullen	16	c Suter	28	c Purchaſe
Booker	10	b Nyren	3	not out
Byes	0	Byes	1	
	115		189	

All England won, by 147 runs.

MOULSEY HURST, *August* 28, 29, 30, 1782.

HAMPSHIRE.

	1ſt inn.	2d inn.
Small	25 b Clifford	14 b Bullen
Nyren	0 c ditto	4 c ditto
Suter	0 c Sir Horace Mann	6 c ditto
Veck	0 b Clifford	26 b ditto
Mann	10 b ditto	10 b Clifford
Duke of Dorſet	0 b ditto	6 c Bullen
	35	66

KENT.

	1ſt inn.	2d inn.
Bullen	1 c Nyren	2 c Nyren
Sir Horace Mann	0 b ditto	1 b ditto
Aylward	20 b Duke of Dorſet	7 b Duke of Dorſet
Clifford	2 b Nyren	7 b ditto
Miller	2 b ditto	2 c Nyren
Brazier	10 c Suter	0 b ditto
	35	19

BOURNE PADDOCK, *September* 16, 17, 18, 19. 1783.

HAMPSHIRE.

	1ſt inn.	2d inn.
Small	8 b Clifford	9 b Bullen
Taylor	2 b Bullen	1 b ditto
Suter	0 b ditto	5 b ditto
Mann	19 b ditto	8 b ditto
Veck	16 b Brazier	32 c Clifford
Harris	1 b ditto	0 b ditto
	46	55

ALL ENGLAND.

	1ſt inn.	2d inn.
Bullen	2 b Harris	0 c Veck
Brazier	11 c Suter	5 b Harris
Aylward	1 b Taylor	7 b ditto
Clifford	2 b ditto	10 b ditto
Bedſter	3 b ditto	0 b ditto
Ring	3 b ditto	26 run out
	22	48

SEVENOAKS,
1783.

East-Kent, ag. West-Kent, (3 men given) Lumpy not to bowl.

JUNE 25, 26.

EAST-KENT.

	1st inn.		2d inn.	
Clifford	22	c Booker	17	c Bowra
Hosmer	3	c Harris	1	c Boreman
Stanford	9	b Bedster	1	c Bowra
Aylward	26	b Boreman	25	b Bullen
Ring	6	b Bullen	1	b ditto
Miller	7	c Boreman	11	c Bowra
Martin	0	not out		
B. Rimmington	3	b Harris	1	not out
T. Pattenden	52	b Boreman	7	c Couchman
W. Pattenden	4	c Harris	18	not out
Amherst	12	b Brazier	2	b Bullen
Byes	3	Byes	2	
	147		86	

WEST-KENT.

	1st inn.		2d inn.	
Harris	10	not out	6	c Stanford
Lumpy	0	b Clifford	5	c Clifford
Bedster	14	c Aylward	43	c Aylward
Bullen	0	b Martin	31	c Clifford
Brazier	5	b ditto	6	c Pattenden
Booker	3	b ditto	12	c ditto
Townsend	9	c ditto	8	b Martin
Couchman	3	c Amherst	9	b ditto
Louch	24	b Martin	1	b Clifford
Boreman	0	c W. Pattenden	12	not out
Bowra	28	b Martin	1	b Clifford
Byes	1	Byes	1	
	97		135	

East-Kent won, by 2 wickets.

WINDMILL DOWNS, 1783.

Kent, (with Bedſter and Yalden) *againſt all England.*

JULY 8, 9,

ALL-ENGLAND.

	1ſt inn.		2d inn.	
Harris	10	b Bullen	0	run out
Bayley	2	c Duke of Dorſet	12	c Ring
Veck	4	c Clifford	3	c Yalden
Small	1	run out	8	b Bullen
Suter	42	b Bullen	3	c Yalden
Taylor	51	b ditto	3	c Bowra
N. Mann	9	b ditto	13	b Bullen
Francis	0	c Clifford	1	b Clifford
Purchaſe	1	c Bullen	4	c ditto
Nyren	4	c Clifford	5	not out
Lumpy	2	not out	1	c Aylward
Byes	14	Byes	9	
	140		62	

KENT.

	1ſt inn.		2d inn.	
Bullen	9	run out	11	c Bayley
Clifford	5	b Harris	0	b Lumpy
Miller	11	b Lumpy	11	c Suter
Aylward	21	b Francis	27	hit wicket
Bedſter	0	b Harris	0	c Purchaſe
Ring	3	b Lumpy	1	c Suter
Bowra	16	c Francis	11	b Lumpy
Duke of Dorſet	8	b ditto	4	c Taylor
Brazier	27	c Suter	10	c Small
Pattenden	0	c Small	14	c Francis
Yalden	9	not out	0	not out
Byes	2	Byes	2	
	111		91	

A Tye Game. § Kent actually won this Match. It was diſcovered afterwards that Pratt, the Scorer, (whoſe method was to cut a notch on a ſtick for every run, and to cut every tenth notch longer, in order to count the whole more expeditiouſly,) had, by miſtake, marked in one place the 11th notch inſtead of the 10th. The ſtick was afterwards produced, but the other ſcorer could not, or would not produce his. The Playing was excellent on both ſides, and the game was ſaved by Clifford's attention. Both ſides were alternately the favorite, & high odds laid.

BOURNE PADDOCK,
1783.

Kent, (with two men) *againſt Hampſhire*, (with two men)

AUGUST 6, 7, 8, 9.

KENT.

	1ſt inn.		2d inn.	
Duke of Dorſet	1	b Lumpy	4	c Taylor
Clifford	0	b ditto	2	not out
Aylward	5	b ditto	7	b Harris
Brazier	0	c Purchaſe	1	run out
Bullen	11	b Harris	22	c Taylor
Bowra	5	b Lumpy	6	b Lumpy
Bedſter	61	c Suter	5	run out
Yalden	7	c Small	2	c Lumpy
Pattenden	22	b Lumpy	0	b Harris
Ring	82	c Francis	4	c ditto
Miller	2	not out	9	c Taylor
Byes	8	Byes	0	
	204		62	

HAMPSHIRE.

	1ſt inn.		2d inn.	
Francis	17	b Clifford	4	c Brazier
Bayley	25	b Bullen	0	b Bullen
Taylor	5	c Clifford	66	b Bullen
N. Mann	11	b ditto	0	c Clifford
Suter	0	b ditto	36	c Bedſter
Small	52	c Yalden	5	c Bowra
Purchaſe	2	b Clifford	0	c Clifford
Veck	9	b Bullen	31	c Bullen
Harris	12	c Bullen	15	not out
Lumpy	0	b Clifford	0	b Aylward
Nyren	18	not out	25	b Brazier
Byes	9	Byes	10	
	160	*H*	192	

Hampſhire won by 86 runs.

WINDMILL DOWNS,
1783.

Hampshire, (with Lumpy and Wells) *against all England.*

AUGUST 26, 27, 28, 29.

HAMPSHIRE.

	1st inn.		2d inn.	
Small	78	run out	13	run out
Mann	18	c Yalden	32	b Brazier
Taylor	16	b Brazier		
Veck	13	b Bullen	14	b Bullen
Suter	54	c Ring		
Francis	0	b Bullen	0	b Brazier
Nyren	21	b ditto		
Purchase	0	c Duke of Dorset	0	c Bullen
Wells	4	b Brazier	2	not out
Harris	7	c Bullen		
Lumpy	0	not out		
Byes	6	Byes	2	
	217		63	

ALL-ENGLAND.

	1st inn.		2d inn.	
Aylward	18	hit wicket	18	c Taylor
Brazier	79	c Small	9	b Harris
Ring	7	b Harris	27	c Taylor
Bedster	15	b Lumpy	6	c ditto
Clifford	19	c Nyren	0	c Harris
Duke of Dorset	3	b Lumpy	3	c Francis
Booker	25	b ditto	21	b Lumpy
Townsend	14	b Francis	22	c Taylor
Wood	7	not out	5	c Small
Yalden	22	c Lumpy	11	not out
Bullen	6	b Harris	9	b Harris
Byes	3	Byes	2	
	218		133	

This match was put off on account of bad weather, never finish'd.

SEVENOAKS,

1784.

Hampshire, (with Lumpy) *against all England.*

JUNE 1, 2.

ALL-ENGLAND.

	1st inn.		2d. inn.	
Bullen	14	b Francis		
Clifford	31	c ditto	0	b Lumpy
Hosmer	2	run out	11	b Francis
Ring	0	b Francis	5	c Taylor
Aylward	37	b ditto	28	not out
Bedster	0	c Taylor	18	not out
Brazier	8	b Lumpy		
Davison	0	b Francis		
Bowra	3	c ditto		
Booker	20	not out		
Townsend	7	c Nyren		
Byes	2	Byes	1	
	124		63	

HAMPSHIRE.

	1st inn.		2d inn.	
Mann	1	c Bowrà	3	b Clifford
Purchase	0	b Clifford	16	c Bedster
Small	3	b Bullen	38	c Bowra
Suter	35	not out	1	b Bullen
Veck	5	b Bullen	19	b Clifford
Taylor	12	b ditto	15	c Bowra
Francis	1	b ditto	8	c Aylward
Nyren	0	b Clifford	8	c Bullen
Cole	4	c ditto	4	b ditto
Small, jun.	6	b Bullen	0	c Bedster
Lumpy	3	b ditto	1	not out
Byes	0	Byes	3	
	70		116	

All England won, by 7 wickets.

STOKE-DOWNS,
1784.

Hampshire, against Kent,

JULY 26, 27, 28.

HAMPSHIRE.

	1st inn.	2d inn.
Small	0 b Bullen	2 b Bullen
Taylor	2 b ditto	11 b Bedster
Noah Mann	12 b Bedster	8 b Bullen
Francis	7 b Bullen	0 b ditto
H. Walker	1 b ditto	0 b ditto
Veck	7 b Bedster	6 c ditto
	29	27

KENT.

	1st inn.	2d inn.
Bullen	6 b Taylor	12 c Taylor
Aylward	0 b ditto	13 b Francis
Ring	8 b Francis	10 b Mann
Bedster	5 b Taylor	0 b ditto
Booker	16 b Mann	0 b ditto
Cole	2 b Taylor	4 b Francis
	37	39

Kent won, by 20 runs

§ Bullen put out nine of the twelve.

WHITE CONDUIT FIELDS, 1786.

White Conduit Club, against Kent, (six given on each side)

JUNE 22, 23, 24.

WHITE-CONDUIT CLUB.

	1st inn.		2d inn.	
Lenox	10	c Ring	5	b Clifford
Ld. Winchelsea	17	b Bullen	13	c Aylward
Monson	12	c Ring	26	c Clifford
Dampier	3	c Stanford	4	b ditto
Boult	1	c Aylward	1	c Aylward
Mann	0	c Stanford	2	c Bullen
Small	1	b Bullen	49	b Clifford
T. Walker	17	c Aylward	13	c Boreman
Taylor	33	b Clifford	7	c Bullen
Purchase	1	b ditto	0	not out
Lumpy	0	not out	2	b Boreman
Byes	8	Byes	1	
	103		123	

KENT.

	1st inn.		2d inn.	
Stanford	14	c Taylor	21	b Lumpy
Hosmer	26	b Lumpy	25	b ditto
Hussey	0	c Taylor	4	not out
Amherst	15	not out	11	b Lumpy
Hatch	0	b Purchase	7	b ditto
Francis	13	run out	3	c Small
Aylward	2	c Lumpy	5	c Monson
Ring	0	c Ld. Winchelsea	4	b Purchase
Clifford	12	b Lumpy	0	run out
Bullen	26	c Boult	19	c Monson
Boreman	11	c Taylor	1	c Lenox
Byes	2	Byes	0	
	121		100	

White Conduit Club won, by 5 runs.

SEVENOAKS,
1786.

Hamshire, (with Lumpy) *against Kent,*

JUNE 26, 27, 28.

HAMPSHIRE.

	1st inn.		2d inn.	
Ld. Winchelsea	6	run out	5	b Boreman
Lumpy	1	not out	1	not out
Small	11	c Bowra	12	b Boreman
Taylor	2	b Clifford	19	c Bullen
Mann	0	run out	0	run out
Purchase	25	b Bullen	3	c Boreman
T. Walker	43	c Bowra	10	b Clifford
H. Walker	39	b Clifford	24	b Bullen
Souter	3	b Bullen	10	b ditto
Nyren	10	c ditto	2	b ditto
Hawkins	0	b Clifford	3	b Clifford
Byes	3	Byes	0	
	143		89	

KENT.

	1st inn.		2d inn.	
Bullen	27	b Lumpy	4	c H. Walker
Aylward	22	c H. Walker	27	b Lumpy
Ring	1	b Purchase	61	not out
Clifford	4	run out		
Townsend	22	c Small	8	c Taylor
Bowra	28	c Hawkins	3	not out
Brazier	8	b Lumpy	4	c Small
Boreman	2	run out		
Newman	1	b Purchase	1	b Lumpy
Couchman	1	b Lumpy	2	b ditto
Booker	5	not out		
Byes	2	Byes	0	
	123		110	

Kent won by 4 wickets.

WINDMILL DOWNS, 1786.

Kent, againſt all Enlgand.

JULY 13, 14, 15.

ALL ENGLAND.

	1ſt inn.		2d inn.	
H. Walker	66	c Bowra	7	c Bullen
T. Walker	55	b ditto	26	run out
Boult	3	b Clifford	11	b Clifford
Small	8	b Bullen	24	b Boreman
Ld. Winchelſea	6	b Cifford	0	b Bullen
Taylor	5	b Bullen	15	c Aylward
Souter	3	hit the ball twice	0	b Bullen
Hawkins	0	b Clifford	0	b Clifford
Purchaſe	4	b Aylward	6	c Boreman
Mann	4	c Bowra	15	not out
Harris	1	not out	4	not out
Byes	8	Byes	2	
	163		110	

KENT.

	1ſt inn.		2d inn.	
Bullen	23	b Harris	29	b Mann
Crozoer	7	b Purchaſe	9	b Purchaſe
Aylward	19	b Harris	53	c Hawkins
Ring	0	c H. Walker	14	b Harris
Clifford	9	c ditto	1	b Purchaſe
Bowra	6	b Harris	0	b Mann
Townſend	4	b Mann	13	b Purchaſe
Finch	0	b Harris	2	b ditto
Pattenden	5	hit wicket	0	c Mann
Boreman	5	c H. Walker	13	c Souter
Booker	5	not out	55	not out
Byes	0	Byes	0	
	83		189	

All England won, by 1 wicket.

MOULSEY-HURST,
1786.

Sir H. Mann, againſt Lord Winchelſea, Alphabetical Match.

AUGUST 3, 4, 5.

SIR HORACE MANN.

	1ſt inn.		2d inn.	
Aylward	3	b Lumpy	6	c Harris
Bowra	0	b Purchaſe	1	b Lumpy
Crozoer	0	c Taylor	3	c ditto
Clifford	9	c ditto	3	c Taylor
Bullen	0	c ditto	10	b Lumpy
Booker	26	c ditto	39	b Harris
Bedſter	15	c H. Walker	0	not out
Brazier	10	c Fennex	3	b Lumpy
Boult	18	c H. Walker	7	c Taylor
Boreman	18	not out	1	c Small
Amherſt	33	b Lumpy	8	b Purchaſe
Byes	11	Byes	1	
	143		82	

LORD WINCHELSEA.

	1ſt inn.		2d inn.	
Ld. Winchelſea	6	b Clifford	5	c Bowra
Huſſey	19	b Brazier	28	c Brazier
H. Walker	8	b Clifford	21	c Bullen
T. Walker	56	c Bullen	6	b Brazier
Small	6	c Boreman	9	b Boreman
Taylor	6	b Bullen	10	b Clifford
Mann	2	c Amherſt	8	b ditto
Purchaſe	2	c Bedſter	26	b Brazier
Harris	0	b Clifford	0	run out
Lumpy	0	c Brazier	2	not out
Fennex	7	not out	22	b Clifford
Byes	4	Byes	7	
	116		144	

Lord Winchelſea won, by 35 runs.

BOURN PADDOCK,
1786.

White Conduit Club, against Kent, (fix given on each fide.)

AUGUST 8, 9, 10, 11, 12.

KENT.

	1ft inn.		2d inn.	
Bullen	0	b Harris	3	b Harris
Aylward	9	c ditto	1	b ditto
Ring	23	b ditto	0	c Louch
Huffey	0	run out	4	c Taylor
Booker	3	b Lumpy	0	c Louch
Collier	14	b Harris	35	b Harris
Hofmer	17	c Dampier	1	not out
Amherft	39	b Eaft	3	c Louch
Stanford	73	b Taylor	3	b Lumpy
Clifford	7	not out	41	b ditto
Boreman	32	c N. Mann	5	c Louch
Byes	1	Byes	1	
	218		97	

WHITE-CONDUIT CLUB.

	1ft inn.		2d inn.	
T. Walker	95	not out	102	b Bullen
Taylor	8	b Bullen	117	b ditto
Small	22	c Hofmer	19	b ditto
Ld. Winchelfea	3	c Clifford	5	c Boreman
N. Mann	6	b Boreman	1	c Bullen
Dampier	3	b Clifford	16	b Clifford
Louch	3	b ditto	9	run out
Eaft	26	b ditto	7	run out
Harris	5	c Hofmer	7	run out
Hawkins	0	c ditto	3	b Bullen
Lumpy	9	b Clifford	3	not out
Byes	3	Byes	7	
	183	I	296	

White Conduit Club won, by 164 runs.

BOURNE PADDOCK, 1786.

Hampſhire, againſt Kent.

SEPTEMBER 6, 7, 8, 9.

HAMPSHIRE.

	1ſt inn.		2d inn.	
T. Walker	26	c Brazier	12	b Bullen
Noah Mann	0	b Bullen	7	b Clifford
Small	3	b ditto	10	c Clifford
Taylor	15	c ditto	0	b Bullen
H. Walker	0	b ditto	7	c ditto
Harris	1	b ditto	3	b ditto
	45		39	

KENT.

	1ſt inn.		2d inn.	
Brazier	4	b Taylor	1	b Harris
Booker	0	b Harris	0	b ditto
Bullen	4	b ditto	2	b ditto
Clifford	0	b ditto	4	b Taylor
Ring	11	b Taylor	57	c Taylor
Aylward	0	hit his wicket	2	not out
	19		66	

Kent won, by 1 wicket.

In the 1ſt innings, T. Walker was in nearly 5 hours. In the 2d innings, when Ring went in, 59 runs were wanting, he got 15 that afternoon, and the next morning, when he went in, he had the promiſe of a conſiderable preſent, if he won the match, himſelf; but unfortunately he got only 42 more, making in all 57. Aylward (the laſt man) went in for the 2 runs, and before he had got one, he gave Taylor a fair catch at the point of the bat, which he miſſed; he had 64 balls before he got 1 run, and 30 before he got the other. Harris bowled the laſt 140 balls to Ring, who played in a maſterly ſtyle throughout the innings.

Clifford bowled 190 balls to T. Walker, without changing.

MARY-LE-BONE,
1787.

Five of W. Conduit Club(with 6 picked men)*againſt all England*.

JUNE 20, 21, 22.

WHITE-CONDUIT CLUB.

	1ſt inn.		2d inn.	
Ld. Winchelſea	3	b Beldam	9	run out
Sir Peter Burrell	0	c Stanford	10	b Mann
Huſſey	21	b Beldam	12	b ditto
Dampier	26	b Bullen	13	b Bullen
Drummond	1	c Hoſmer	1	c Beldam
Harris	5	not out	2	not out
Clifford	6	run out	0	b Purchaſe
Ring	18	c Bullen	2	b Beldam
Taylor	12	c ditto	25	c Mann
T. Walker	11	c ditto	11	b Beldam
H. Walker	0	run out	5	c Amherſt
Byes	9	Byes	3	
	112		93	

ALL-ENGLAND.

	1ſt inn.		2d inn.	
Amherſt	20	not out	18	c H. Walker
Hoſmer	41	c H. Walker	2	c ditto
Stanford	0	b ditto	0	c ditto
Bullen	14	b Harris	0	b Clifford
Aylward	94	run out	15	ſtumpt out
Small, ſen.	30	b Taylor	32	not out
Purchaſe	0	b Harris	3	c Taylor
Beldam	17	b Clifford	63	run out
John Wells	8	b Harris	12	c Clifford
Small, jun.	3	c Clifford	42	c ditto
Mann	11	b Harris	6	c Huſſey
Byes	9	Byes	4	
	247		197	

All England won, by 239 runs.

MARY-LE-BONE, 1787.

Kent, againſt Hampſhire.

AUGUST 2, 3, 4.

KENT.

	1ſt inn.		2d inn.	
Bullen	5	b Harris	0	b Harris
Bowra	1	b ditto	0	b ditto
Ring	24	b ditto	1	b ditto
Aylward	0	b ditto	2	b ditto
Clifford	14	b ditto	1	b ditto
Brazier	9	b Noah Mann	9	b ditto
	53		13	

HAMPSHIRE.

	1ſt inn.		2d inn.	
Small	9	b Clifford	0	b Brazier
Harris	0	b Clifford	1	b Bullen
T. Walker	4	b Bullen	5	b Brazier
H. Walker	7	b Clifford	0	b Brazier
Noah Mann	6	b ditto	4	b Bullen
Taylor	1	b ditto	6	c Booker †
	27		16	

Kent won, by 23 runs.

† Booker ſtood out ſome time for Bowra, who was hurt.

COXHEATH,

1787.

Kent, againſt all England.

AUGUST 7, 8, 9, 10.

ALL-ENGLAND.

	1ſt inn.		2d inn.	
Ld. Winchelſea	5	b Brazier	5	run out
T. Walker	57	run out	1	run out
H. Walker	22	b Bullen	23	b Bullen
Taylor	36	b ditto	9	not out
Mann	18	not out		
Small, ſen.	15	b Brazier	4	b Brazier
Small, jun.	3	b Clifford	10	c Hoſmer
James Wells	1	b ditto	0	not out
John Wells	36	b ditto	3	b Bullen
Beldam	42	b ditto	14	c Clifford
Purchaſe	14	run out	7	b Brazier
Byes	7	Byes	3	
	256		79	

KENT.

	1ſt inn.		2d inn.	
Huſſey	0	c Small, ſen.	7	c Taylor
Amherſt	18	c Taylor	6	c Beldam
Hoſmer	5	b ditto	10	c Small, ſen.
Aylward	3	run out	8	c Beldam
Ring	16	b Taylor	4	ſtumpt out
Clifford	50	b ditto	23	c John Wells
Brazier	25	b Purchaſe	39	c H. Walker
Croſoer	14	b ditto	39	c ditto
Stanford	1	c Ld. Winchelſea	9	run out
Pilcher	6	b Purchaſe	7	c Beldam
Bullen	1	not out	39	not out
Byes	1	Byes	3	
	140		194	

All England won, by 2 wickets.

BOURNE PADDOCK, 1787.

Hampshire, against all England.

AUGUST 14, 15, 16.

HAMPSHIRE.

	1st inn.		2d inn.	
Purchase	6	b Clifford	0	run out
Small, sen.	40	b Fennix	24	b Boreman
Taylor	8	b Clifford	20	run out
T. Walker	65	c Bullen	17	b Fennix
H. Walker	2	b Clifford	10	c Brazier
N. Mann	4	b Fennix	12	b Bullen
John Wells	10	b Clifford	13	b Fennix
Small, jun.	0	b ditto	10	not out
Ld. Winchelsea	12	b Fennix	20	c Amherst
Beldam	28	run out	42	b Fennix
Harris	8	not out	3	b Clifford
Byes	10	Byes	3	
	193		174	

ALL-ENGLAND.

	1st inn.		2d inn.	
Clifford	5	c Small, jun.	3	b Harris
Bullen	0	c Beldam	1	c Ld. Winchelsea
Fennix	0	b Harris	9	b Harris
Ring	24	b ditto	13	run out
Brazier	21	c Beldam	0	c H. Walker
Crosoer	0	b Harris	2	b Harris
Amherst	0	c N. Mann	3	c Wells
Aylward	2	b Taylor	0	c T. Walker
Boreman	0	b Harris	0	not out
Louch	4	c Taylor	0	c Purchase
Booker	0	not out	7	run out
Byes	4	Byes	3	
	60		41	

Hampshire won by 266 runs.

BOURNE PADDOCK,
1787.
ALPHABETICAL MATCH.
AUGUST 28, 29, 30, 31.

SIR HORACE MANN.

	1st inn.		2d inn.	
T. Walker	4	run out	3	b Harris
H. Walker	8	b Harris	5	c Taylor
Small, sen.	8	b Clifford	57	c Bullen
Ring	7	hit wicket	2	c Clifford
Fennix	8	c Louch	8	b Taylor
Small, jun.	0	b Clifford	13	b ditto
John Wells	10	b Taylor	0	b ditto
Purchase	1	b ditto	8	b ditto
Aylward	28	b Bullen	35	b ditto
James Wells	1	not out	1	b Harris
Lumpy	3	b Harris	2	not out
Byes	4	Byes	4	
	82		138	

LORD WINCHELSEA.

	1st inn.		2d inn.	
Bedster	3	c John Wells	1	c Fennix
Brazier	18	c Fennix	19	c ditto
Beldam	1	run out	22	run out
Bullen	6	run out	29	b Lumpy
Taylor	6	c John Wells	14	c Fennix
Clifford	4	c Lumpy	0	c ditto
Booker	10	b ditto	36	b ditto
Louch	1	b Fennix	28	run out
Lord	11	b ditto	2	c Fennix
N. Mann	28	c H. Walker	4	b ditto
Harris	0	not out	0	not out
Byes	6	Byes	0	
	94		155	

Lord Winchelsea won, by 29 runs.

WINDMILL DOWNS, 1787.

Hampshire, against all England.

SEPTEMBER 3, 4, 5.

ALL-ENGLAND.

	1st inn.		2d. inn.	
Aylward	31	c Purchase	65	c John Wells
Clifford	3	b Taylor	2	b Beldam
Ring	14	c Taylor	2	c H. Walker
Pilcher	0	c Taylor	13	run out
Brazier	3	b Harris	14	c John Wells
Fennix	2	b Harris	0	c Taylor
Booker	1	c Beldam	15	run out
Louch	21	not out	8	c Mann
Bullen	2	c Small	2	not out
Boreman	23	c Beldam	0	b Mann
Nyren jun.	3	c John Wells	1	c Taylor
Byes	6	Byes	1	
	109		123	

HAMPSHIRE.

	1st inn.		2d inn.	
T. Walker	7	b Boreman	1	b Boreman
Small	3	c Aylward	7	b Bullen
Taylor	1	run out	5	b Bullen
H. Walker	1	b Bullen	2	b ditto
Beldam	0	c Boreman	0	run out
John Wells	6	run out	23	run out
Noah Mann	5	b Bullen	41	c Bullen
Small, jun.	4	run out	4	b Boreman
Purchase	0	run out	30	not out
Harris	4	not out	4	b Bullen
James Wells	1	b Bullen	5	run out
Byes	5	Byes	8	
	37		130	

All England won, by 65 runs.

MARY-LE-BONE,

1787.

Sir H. Mann, againſt Lord Winchelſea, Alphabetical Match.

SEPTEMBER 10, 11, 12.

LORD WINCHELSEA.

	1ſt inn.		2d inn.	
Beldam	6	run out	0	b Purchaſe
Booker	12	b Lumpy	22	b Lumpy
Boreman	8	c John Wells	3	c Aylward
Brazier	3	b Lumpy	0	c Small, ſen.
Louch	3	c H. Walker	3	c John Wells
Taylor	23	not out	6	b Lumpy
Bullen	3	c Small, jun.	11	c Small, ſen.
Clifford	17	c Pilcher	8	b Lumpy
Noah Mann	1	b Lumpy	5	c Purchaſe
Boult	1	run out	3	not out
Harris	0	c Lumpy	0	b Purchaſe
Byes	7	Byes	0	
	84		61	

SIR HORACE MANN.

	1ſt inn.		2d inn.	
Aylward	0	c Clifford	15	b Boreman
Small, ſen.	8	run out	26	b Clifford
T. Walker	6	b Harris	40	b Harris
Ring	26	b Clifford	3	c Beldam
H. Walker	44	b Bullen	5	c Bullen
John Wells	19	b Brazier	11	b Harris
Fennix	1	run out	1	c ditto
Purchaſe	0	hit wicket	11	not out
Small, jun.	1	b Bullen	4	c Louch
Pilcher	4	not out	0	c Clifford
Lumpy	0	b Brazier	1	b Brazier
Byes	7	Byes	6	
	116		123	

Sir Horace Mann won, by 94 runs.

MARY-LE-BONE,

1788.

ALPHABETICAL MATCH.

MAY 26, 27, 28.

LORD WINCHELSEA.

	1st inn.		2d inn.	
S. Amherst, Esq.	2	b Purchase	7	c Ring
Hosmer, Esq.	1	b ditto	22	b Fennix
G. Louch, Esq.	1	c Pilcher	15	b Lumpy
Booker	16	b Purchase	11	b ditto
Bullen	8	c H. Walker	15	c Small, sen.
Brazier	7	b Lumpy	6	c Fennix
Beldam	14	c H. Walker	3	b Lumpy
Clifford	1	b Purchase	5	c ditto
Harris	1	not out	1	run out
Noah Mann	0	run out	4	not out
Taylor	6	c Fennix	1	c Ld. Winchelsea
Byes	0	Byes	2	
	57		92	

SIR HORACE MANN.

	1st inn.		2d inn.	
Ld. Winchelsea	7	b Bullen	6	b Harris
Stevens	5	not out	9	b ditto
Small, sen.	19	b Harris	24	c Taylor
Small, jun.	3	c Beldam	4	b Harris
T. Walker	6	b Harris	19	b ditto
H. Walker	12	c Bullen	6	b ditto
Purchase	24	b ditto	12	c Louch
Fennix	0	b Harris	25	not out
Pilcher	1	b Clifford	9	b Harris
Ring	4	b Harris	12	c Louch
Aylward	7	b Clifford	18	b Brazier
Byes	14	Byes	9	
	102		153	

Sir Horace Mann won, by 106 runs

MARY-LE-BONE,

1788.

Mr. PAWLET, againſt Mr. EAST, ſelect Elevens.

JUNE 5, 6, 7.

MR. PAWLET.

	1ſt inn.		2d inn.	
T. Walker	35	c Purchaſe	2	c Louch
H. Walker	5	c Ingram	13	c Beldam
Bullen	13	c Harris	1	not out
Brazier	15	not out	6	c Beldam
Clifford	1	c Amherſt	29	c Louch
Aylward	8	b Purchaſe	28	c Ingram
Ring	7	c Amherſt	20	c Purchaſe
Bowra	3	b Harris	2	c Louch
Small, ſen.	8	c Purchaſe	3	c Purchaſe
Taylor	1	c Louch	2	c Louch
Noah Mann	7	c Purchaſe	18	b Harris
Byes	3	Byes	6	
	106		130	

MR. EAST.

	1ſt inn.		2d inn.	
G. Eaſt, Eſq.	0	c Aylward	0	c Aylward
G. Louch, Eſq.	1	not out	1	c Bowra
S. Amherſt, Eſq.	2	run out	1	b Clifford
Hoſmer, Eſq.	0	b Clifford	9	b ditto
Harris	2	b ditto	8	b ditto
Ingram	40	b Brazier	7	not out
Beldam	5	b Clifford	5	b Mann
John Wells	6	b Brazier	11	ſtumpt Taylor
Small, jun.	12	b Clifford	7	c Taylor
Booker	11	b ditto	0	c Bullen
Purchaſe	46	b Brazier	18	c ditto
Byes	15	Byes	4	
	140		71	

Mr. Pawlet won by 25 runs.

MOULSEY-HURST,

1788.

LORD WINCHELSEA, against Mr. A. SMITH.

JUNE 9, 10.

MR. A. SMITH.

	1st inn.		2d inn.	
Hon. C. Monſon	0	b Butcher	4	c Wells
A. Smith, Eſq.	0	c Beldam	5	b Butcher
Drummond, Eſq.	0	b Butcher	0	c H. Walker
G. Talbot, Eſq.	6	not out	1	c Ld. Winchelſea
Small, ſen.	6	b Lumpy	23	c H. Walker
Nyren	3	b ditto	9	b Lumpy
Small, jun.	7	b Butcher	1	c Wells
Noah Mann	7	b ditto	11	b Lumpy
Purchaſe	24	b ditto	4	b Butcher
Taylor	3	c Beldam	4	b ditto
Harris	0	b Lumpy	0	not out
Byes	3	Byes	1	
	59		63	

LORD WINCHELSEA.

	1st inn.		2d inn.	
Ld. Winchelſea	6	b Purchaſe	0	b Harris
Ld. Strathaven	2	c ditto		
H. Fitzroy, Eſq.	0	b Mann		
Field	22	c Purchaſe		
H. Walker	14	c Taylor	16	not out
T. Walker	5	c Drummond	17	not out
Butcher	11	c Smith		
Beldam	10	c Taylor		
John Wells	14	b Harris		
Davie	0	c Purchaſe		
Lumpy	0	not out		
Byes	6	Byes	0	
	90		33	

Mr. A. Smith won, by 9 wickets.

STOKE-DOWNS,
1788.

Hampſhire, againſt all England.

JUNE 17, 18.

HAMPSHIRE.

	1ſt inn.		2d inn.
T. Walker	6	run out	
H. Walker	23	b Clifford	
Small, ſen.	3	run out	
Small, jun.	5	b Lumpy	
Taylor	22	c Ingram	
Beldam	52	not out	
John Wells	39	b Bullen	
Purchaſe	3	b Clifford	
Harris	21	b Fennix	
Noah Mann	0	c Clifford	
James Wells	37	b Lumpy	
Byes	9		
	220		

ALL-ENGLAND.

	1ſt inn.		2d inn.	
Aylward	30	b Purchaſe	5	b Purchaſe
Louch, Eſq.	2	c Harris	0	c Mann
Bullen	0	run out	7	b Purchaſe
Clifford	0	c James Wells	15	not out
Ring	6	b Harris	6	b Purchaſe
Cole	1	c Mann	1	b Harris
Fennix	0	b Harris	18	run out
Booker	5	run out	2	b Harris
Boreman	17	c Taylor	19	c Taylor
Lumpy	1	not out	2	b Harris
Ingram	1	b Purchaſe	5	run out
Byes	0	Byes	1	
	63		81	

Hampſhire won, by one innings, and 76 runs.

PERRAM-DOWNS,
1788.

Lord Winchelsea, against Mr. A. Smith.

JULY 3, 4, 5.

LORD WINCHELSEA.

	1st inn.		2d inn.	
T. Walker	17	b Mann	0	b Harris
H. Walker	78	b Taylor	10	run out
John Wells	5	b Harris	3	c Mann
Beldam	59	b ditto	8	c A. Smith
Field	10	run out	5	b Mann
Ld. Winchelsea	2	b Taylor	5	b Taylor
Drummond	0	b Harris	6	b Mann
Fitzroy	5	b ditto	0	b ditto
Davie	16	not out	4	not out
Butcher	6	b Mann	0	b Harris
Lumpy	2	b ditto	0	b Mann
Byes	3	Byes	3	
	203		44	

MR. A. SMITH.

	1st inn.		2d inn.	
Small, jun.	8	c Beldam	21	c Lumpy
Horsey	1	b Butcher		
Small, sen.	4	c Wells	7	c Wells
Purchase	14	b Butcher	43	not out
Taylor	2	b ditto	22	c Beldam
Noah Mann	41	not out		
A. Smith, Esq.	8	b Butcher	4	b Butcher
Talbot	28	b Beldam	8	not out
Stewart	2	c ditto	3	c Davie
Hunt	0	b ditto	29	b Lumpy
Harris	1	b Butcher		
Byes	1	Byes	1	
	110		138	

Mr. A. Smith won, by 4 wickets.

MOULSEY-HURST,
1788.

Surry, (with Harris) *againſt Kent*.

JULY 15, 16, 17, 18.

SURRY.

	1ſt inn.		2d inn.
Ld. Winchelſea	0	b Boreman	
T. Walker	93	not out	
H. Walker	9	b Bullen	
Beldam	3	run out	
John Wells	7	b Brazier	
James Wells	1	c Pilcher	
Souter	17	c Clifford	
Ingram	0	c Bullen	
Butcher	14	c ditto	
Harris	44	b Boreman	
Lumpy	3	c Sir P. Burrell	
Byes	6		
	197		

KENT.

	1ſt inn.		2d. inn.	
Sir Peter Burrell	19	c Lumpy	0	b Lumpy
Amherſt, Eſq.	1	c Harris	0	c H. Walker
Hoſmer	1	c H. Walker	1	c ditto
Bullen	4	b Harris	5	run out
Clifford	17	b Lumpy	11	b Lumpy
Aylward	17	not out	0	c John Wells
Francis	1	b Lumpy	0	b Harris
Brazier	0	b ditto	17	c ditto
Boreman	0	b ditto	12	b Lumpy
Booker	20	b ditto	0	b Harris
Pilcher	0	c H. Walker	5	not out
Byes	1	Byes	0	
	81		51	

Surry won, by one innings and 65 runs.

SEVENOAKS,

1788.

Hampshire, against all England.

JULY 24, 25.

HAMPSHIRE.

	1st inn.		2d inn.	
T. Walker	5	b Lumpy	9	c Clifford
H. Walker	8	c Louch	31	c ditto
Small, sen.	10	c Clifford	3	c ditto
Ld. Winchelsea	2	not out	4	c Lumpy
John Wells	0	c Aylward	29	b ditto
James Wells	12	c Louch	0	b ditto
Taylor	7	c Bowra	3	b Fennix
Beldam	7	c Clifford	6	b Lumpy
Purchase	7	b ditto	8	not out
Harris	2	b ditto	0	b Clifford
Noah Mann	15	c Bowra	5	b ditto
Byes	0	Byes	4	
	75		102	

ALL-ENGLAND.

	1st inn.		2d inn.	
Louch	35	b Taylor	0	c John Wells
Aylward	4	c Beldam	4	b Mann
Clifford	6	b Purchase	10	run out
Bullen	1	c Taylor	2	not out
Booker	0	run out	7	c H. Walker
Brazier	2	b Harris	1	c Purchase
Fennix	13	b Taylor	2	c Taylor
Bowra	5	run out	1	b Mann
Boreman	9	c H. Walker	6	b ditto
Lumpy	3	not out	0	c Beldam
Crawte	12	run out	0	b Mann
Byes	1	Byes	0	
	91		33	

Hampshire won, by 53 runs.

COXHEATH,
1788.

Kent, againſt all England.

JULY 29, 30, 31.

KENT.

	1ſt inn.		2d inn.	
Amherſt, Eſq.	8	c Louch	28	b T. Walker
Hoſmer	10	c ditto	2	b Harris
Clifford	10	c ditto	2	b ditto
Aylward	11	c ditto	0	c Fennix
Ring	1	c Small, ſen.	16	b Harris
Boreman	0	b Purchaſe	0	c Louch
Bullen	1	not out	3	not out
Brazier	7	b Purchaſe	0	b Harris
Booker	8	run out	17	c Hunt
Small	1	c Annett	1	c Annett
Nicholſon	0	b Harris	2	c Louch
Byes	4	Byes	0	
	61		71	

ALL-ENGLAND.

	1ſt inn.		2d inn.
T. Walker	31	c Small	
Louch	10	b Boreman	
Small, ſen.	27	c Aylward	
Small, jun.	11	b Clifford	
Harris	13	b ditto	
Purchaſe	44	c Boreman	
Taylor	9	b Bullen	
Fennix	14	c Small	
Noah Mann	39	not out	
Hunt	7	c Aylward	
Annett	2	b Bullen	
Byes	5		
	212		

All England won, by one innings, and 80 runs.

BOURN PADDOCK,
1788.

Surry, (with Harris) *againſt Kent.*

AUGUST 5, 6, 7.

SURRY.

	1ſt inn.		2d inn.	
Ld. Winchelſea	8	c Fennix	0	b Boreman
Beldam	49	b Brazier	33	b Clifford
Butcher	1	b Boreman	9	not out
Crawte	11	not out	0	b Clifford
Lumpy	9	c Aylward	0	b ditto
Souter	9	b Clifford	0	b ditto
T. Walker	13	c Amherſt	0	b Boreman
H. Walker	8	c Bowra	16	b Clifford
John Wells	18	b Clifford	3	c Bullen
James Wells	2	c Amherſt	9	c Brazier
Harris	30	b Clifford	6	b ditto
Byes	15	Byes	1	
	173		77	

KENT.

	1ſt inn.		2d inn.	
Amherſt, Eſq.	11	c Souter	7	b Lumpy
Aylward	31	c Crawte	2	c Butcher
Bullen	15	b Lumpy	0	c Butcher
Booker	16	run out	6	c H. Walker
Brazier	12	c John Wells	31	not out
Boreman	4	not out	9	c Lumpy
Bowra	0	run out	6	c Beldam
Clifford	9	c Beldam	4	c H. Walker
Pilcher	15	b Harris	17	c John Wells
Ring	9	c John Wells	4	c T. Walker
Grinſtead	0	b Lumpy	0	run out
Byes	5	Byes	0	
	127		86	

Surry won, by 37 runs.

WINDMILL DOWNS,
1788.

Surry, against Hampshire.

AUGUST 13, 14, 15.

SURRY.

	1st inn.		2d inn.	
Ld. Winchelsea	10	hit wicket	2	c Louch
Butcher	2	b Purchase	7	not out
T. Walker	0	run out	12	c Neal
H. Walker	12	b Taylor	4	c Taylor
Beldam	14	c Louch	17	b Harris
John Wells	11	hit wicket	6	b ditto
James Wells	7	c Taylor	5	b Mann
Souter	11	b Mann	24	run out
Crawte	3	b Harris	0	b Taylor
Field	2	not out	11	b Mann
Lumpy	0	b Mann	0	b ditto
Byes	8	Byes	7	
	80		95	

HAMPSHIRE.

	1st inn.		2d inn.	
Louch	3	b Lumpy	8	b Beldam
Talbot	7	b Butcher	0	b Butcher
Small, sen.	37	run out	0	b Lumpy
Harris	12	c John Wells		
Noah Mann	18	b Lumpy		
Purchase	2	b Butcher		
Neal	0	c John Wells	4	b Butcher
Small, jun.	17	c Ld. Winchelsea	22	b Lumpy
Taylor	1	b Butcher	12	c H. Walker
Annett	6	b Lumpy	2	not out
Freemantle	5	not out	9	not out
Byes	6	Byes	5	
	114		62	

Hampshire won, by 4 wickets.

MARY-LE-BONE,
1788.

Hampſhire, againſt all England.

AUGUST 21, 22.

ALL-ENGLAND.

	1ſt inn.		2d inn.	
Ld. Winchelſea	3	b Mann	7	b Taylor
Bullen	0	b ditto	4	b Harris
T. Walker	4	b Harris	5	b ditto
Beldam	0	b ditto	3	b ditto
Butcher	0	b ditto	0	c ditto
Fennix	1	b ditto	0	b ditto
	8		19	

HAMPSHIRE.

	1ſt inn.		2d inn.	
Talbot	0	b Fennix	0	b Bullen
Small, ſen.	7	b ditto		
Purchaſe	12	c T. Walker		
Harris	1	b Bullen		
Noah Mann	1	b ditto	4	not out
Taylor	3	b Fennix		
	24		4	

Hampſhire won, by 5 wickets.

BOURNE PADDOCK,
1788.
ALPHABETICAL MATCH.
AUGUST 26, 27, 28, 29.

SIR HORACE MANN.

	1st inn.		2d inn.	
Clifford	0	c Purchase	15	c Purchase
Bullen	7	run out	0	not out
Brazier	7	c Fennix	11	c Lumpy
Noah Mann	0	c Small, jun.	28	c John Wells
Beldam	45	c Aylward	51	c Small, sen.
Taylor	0	b Lumpy	0	b H. Walker
Amherst, Esq.	20	b Fennix	22	c Purchase
Louch	9	b Lumpy	7	c H. Walker
Booker	0	b Lumpy	0	b Purchase
Harris	3	b Fennix	0	b Lumpy
Crawte	0	not out	6	c H. Walker
Byes	3	Byes	1	
	94		141	

LORD WINCHELSEA.

	1st inn.		2d inn.	
H. Walker	0	b Harris	0	c Beldam
Fennix	0	b Bullen	3	not out
T. Walker	7	b Harris	17	c Bullen
Purchase	4	c Taylor	17	b Brazier
Small, sen.	12	b Clifford	15	c Taylor
John Wells	23	c N. Mann	4	b Harris
Small, jun.	0	b Harris	0	c ditto
James Wells	0	b Taylor	0	c Clifford
Windsor	1	c Beldam	0	c Beldam
Aylward	48	b Taylor	2	c Bullen
Lumpy	0	not out	1	c Clifford
Byes	5	Byes	1	
	100		60	

Sir Horace Mann won, by 75 runs.

BOURNE PADDOCK,

1788.

Kent, against Hampshire.

AUGUST 29, 30, SEPTEMBER 1, 2, 3.

KENT.

	1st inn.	2d inn.
Aylward	1 b Harris	6 b Harris
Brazier	0 b ditto	5 c Small, jun.
Clifford	1 b Taylor	1 b Harris
Bullen	0 c Purchase	1 b ditto
Booker	0 b Harris	10 b Purchase
Ring	2 b Taylor	9 b Harris
	4	32

HAMPSHIRE.

	1st inn.	2d inn.
Purchase	6 c Brazier	2 b Bullen
Small, sen.	1 b ditto	3 b ditto
Small, jun.	2 b Bullen	2 b Clifford
Noah Mann	8 c Brazier	8 b ditto
Taylor	7 c ditto	1 b Bullen
Harris	1 b Bullen	1 b Clifford
	25	17

Hampshire won, by 6 runs.

MARY-LE-BONE,

1789.

ALPHABETICAL MATCH.

JUNE 3,—15, 16.

SIR HORACE MANN.

	1ſt inn.		2d inn.	
Clifford	0	b Purchaſe	19	b Fennix
Brazier	23	c John Wells	3	b Purchaſe
Beldam	7	c ditto	44	c John Wells
Bullen	5	b Purchaſe	11	b Lumpy
Louch	5	c ditto	7	b Purchaſe
Col. Lenox	7	b ditto	15	not out
Taylor	2	b Lumpy	3	c Purchaſe
Noah Mann	0	c ditto	48	b ditto
Ingram	1	b Purchaſe	0	c Small, ſen.
Amherſt, Eſq.	1	not out	0	b Lumpy
Harris	0	run out	1	b ditto
Byes	0	Byes	3	
	51		154	

LORD WINCHELSEA.

	1ſt inn.		2d inn.	
Ld. Winchelſea	0	b Beldam	21	not out
Purchaſe	40	b Beldam	1	b Brazier
Small, ſen.	44	c Clifford	19	run out
T. Walker	29	b ditto	31	b Beldam
H. Walker	0	b Harris	5	c ditto
John Wells	35	c Clifford	48	c Brazier
Aylward	0	b Beldam	7	b Clifford
Lumpy	2	b ditto	0	b Beldam
Fennix	3	b ditto	7	b Mann
Ring	0	b ditto	24	b ditto
Small, jun.	12	not out	13	b ditto
Byes	3	Byes	1	
	168		177	

Lord Winchelſea won, by 140 runs.

MOULSEY-HURST,
1789.

SURRY, (with Noah Mann) *againſt KENT*.

JUNE 10, 11, 12.

SURRY.

	1ſt inn.		2d. inn.	
Ld. Winchelſea	4	b Clifford	1	b Brazier
Col. Lenox	13	b Bullen	0	b ditto
H. Walker	7	c Boreman	26	c Palmer
T. Walker	50	b Clifford	21	c Crawte
J. Walker	7	b ditto	0	b Clifford
Beldam	0	run out	19	b Brazier
John Wells	15	b Boxall	0	c Clifford
Lumpy	3	b Boreman	3	not out
Butcher	13	not out	3	b Brazier
Souter	3	c Boxall	13	b ditto
Noah Mann	8	c Bullen	0	b Clifford
Byes	0	Byes	1	
	123		87	

KENT.

	1ſt inn.		2d inn.	
Amherſt, Eſq.	3	run out	1	b Lumpy
Boxall	4	b Butcher		
Bullen	15	c Ld. Winchelſea	1	not out
Clifford	11	b T. Walker		
Brazier	6	b Lumpy	45	c John Wells
Ring	0	c Mann	15	b Butcher
Aylward	10	c J. Walker	0	c Lumpy
Boreman	0	ſt. John Wells	1	not out
Crawte	1	c H. Walker	13	run out
Pilcher	24	c John Wells	10	c J. Walker
Palmer	43	not out	8	run out
Byes	0	Byes	0	
	117		94	

Kent won, by 3 wickets.

MARY-LE-BONE,
1789.

Eleven *of Hampſhire*, *againſt* Thirteen *of all England.*

JUNE 26, 27, & JULY 2.

HAMPSHIRE.

	1ſt inn.		2d inn.	
T. Walker	0	b Clifford	0	b Fennix
H. Walker	0	b Boreman		
Purchaſe	39	b ditto		
Taylor	6	b ditto	4	b Boreman
Small, ſen.	2	b ditto	6	not out
John Wells	4	b Clifford	0	b Fennix
Noah Mann	1	b ditto	14	b ditto
Beldam	94	c Brazier	16	not out
James Wells	1	b Clifford		
Small, jun.	1	c Louch		
Harris	0	not out		
Byes	2	Byes	2	
	150		42	

ALL-ENGLAND.

	1ſt inn.		2d inn.	
Ring	0	b Purchaſe	11	b Purchaſe
White	17	b Taylor	7	c John Wells
Pilcher	4	c Beldam	7	b Purchaſe
Palmer	2	b Taylor	0	run out
Aylward	37	b Harris	9	c John Wells
Brazier	9	run out	1	c Beldam
Clifford	4	c Beldam	0	b Purchaſe
Bullen	12	b Harris	2	c Beldam
Fennix	21	c H. Walker	0	run out
Ingram	9	b Harris	33	c Small, jun.
Boreman	0	c Belbam	0	not out
Lumpy	0	not out	0	b Harris
Louch	0	b Purchaſe	2	b ditto
Byes	3	Byes	1	
	118	*M*	73	

Hampſhire won, by 5 wickets.

COXHEATH,

1789.

E. Kent, with Boreman & 4 *of Hants.* v *W. Kent*, & 4 *of Surry.*

JUNE 29, 30.

EAST KENT.

	1ſt inn.		2d inn.	
Harris	11	b Brazier	1	c Wells
Purchaſe	14	c Beldam	0	c H. Walker
Small, ſen.	28	c Wells	4	b Beldam
Taylor	8	c Bullen	2	b ditto
Aylward	25	c Beldam	20	not out
Ring	0	c T. Walker	1	b Beldam
Pilcher	22	run out	0	run out
Boreman	3	c T. Walker	2	b Beldam
Wood	11	b Brazier	0	b Clifford
Bates	0	c Wells	1	run out
Church	2	not out	3	b Clifford
Byes	0	Byes	2	
	124		36	

WEST KENT.

	1ſt inn.		2d inn.	
Amherſt	17	b Harris	9	b Purchaſe
Hoſmer	8	not out	7	run out
Bullen	1	b Harris	5	c Ring
Clifford	4	b ditto	3	not out
Brazier	9	c Purchaſe	0	c Wood
T. Walker	3	b Harris	0	c Purchaſe
H. Walker	0	b ditto	1	c Bates
John Wells	20	c Taylor	5	run out
Beldam	10	b Harris	6	b Harris
Crawte	25	c Ring	6	c Bates
Palmer	6	b Purchaſe	0	c Aylward
Byes	7	Byes	0	
	110		42	

Eaſt-Kent won by 8 runs.

STOKE-DOWNS,
1789.
KENT, againſt HAMPSHIRE.
JULY 9, 10.

KENT.

	1ſt inn.	2d inn.
Aylward	12 b Taylor	2 b Taylor
Pilcher	12 b ditto	10 b Purchaſe
Bullen	0 run out	2 b ditto
Brazier	7 b Taylor	2 b Taylor
Clifford	10 c Small, jun.	18 c ditto
Ring	25 b Taylor	30 b Small, jun.
	66	64

HAMPSHIRE.

	1ſt inn.	2d inn.
Small, ſen.	8 b Bullen	
Purchaſe	6 b Clifford	0 b Bullen
Noah Mann	10 b Clifford	
Freemantle	6 c Bullen	10 b Brazier
Small, jun.	0 b Clifford	
Taylor	1 b Bullen	
	31	10

This match was put off on account of the weather, and never played out.

WINDMILL DOWNS,
1789.

Kent, againſt Hampſhire, (with four Gentlemen)

JULY 13, 14.

KENT.

	1ſt inn.		2d inn.	
Pilcher	0	c Taylor	8	b N. Mann
Aylward	15	run out	15	b Harris
Clifford	26	c Small, jun.	4	c Purchaſe
Brazier	14	b Taylor	2	b Harris
Amherſt	0	c Louch	0	not out
Crawte	1	b Taylor	0	b N. Mann
Ring	4	b Harris	0	b ditto
Talbot	1	c Louch	4	b Purchaſe
Palmer	2	b Harris	0	b N. Mann
Bullen	20	b Purchaſe	0	b Harris
Boreman	14	not out	1	b ditto
Byes	1	Byes	0	
	98		34	

HAMPSHIRE.

	1ſt inn.		2d inn.	
Purchaſe	6	c Clifford	1	c Aylward
Freemantle	11	run out	1	b Clifford
Small, ſen.	0	b Bullen	6	b ditto
Noah Mann	11	b ditto	1	b ditto
Ld. Winchelſea	0	b ditto	0	b Bullen
A. Smith, Eſq.	0	b ditto	3	c Clifford
Small, jun.	3	b Clifford	1	c Amherſt
Louch	0	b ditto	4	c Clifford
Taylor	3	b Bullen	5	not out
Boult	15	b Clifford	3	c Amherſt
Harris	0	not out	0	b Bullen
Byes	0	Byes	2	
	49		27	

Kent won, by 56 runs.

UXBRIDGE,
1789.

Kent, against (five Gentlemen and six others)*of all England.*

JULY 23, 24, 25.

KENT.

	1ſt inn.		2d inn.	
Pilcher	5	c Louch	1	c Boult
Aylward	7	b Harris	23	run out
Clifford	13	b ditto	6	b N. Mann
Brazier	3	b N. Mann	2	b Harris
Ring	6	b ditto	7	b Purchaſe
Amherſt	10	b Purchaſe	7	b N. Mann
Talbot	0	run out	1	b Harris
Bullen	1	c Louch	4	not out
Boreman	18	c Beldam	2	run out
Palmer	4	b Purchaſe	0	b N. Mann
Crawte	19	not out	0	b ditto
Byes	1	Byes	0	
	87		53	

ALL-ENGLAND.

	1ſt inn.		2d inn.
Ld. Winchelſea	0	c Boreman	
Vincent	12	b Clifford	
T. Walker	11	run out	
John Wells	21	hit wicket	
Louch	3	b Boreman	
Boult	13	b Clifford	
Beldam	48	b Bullen	
Purchaſe	6	run out	
Noah Mann	34	b Bullen	
A. Smith	0	not out	
Harris	0	run out	
Byes	2		
	150		

All England won, by one innings, and 10 runs.

COXHEATH,

1789.

E. Kent, (with Boreman & 4 Hants. *ag. W. Kent*, (& 4 of Surry)

AUGUST 4, 5.

EAST-KENT.

	1ſt inn.		2d inn.	
Pilcher	7	b Beldam	2	c Bullen
Purchaſe	13	c H. Walker	11	b Clifford
Smal, ſen.	13	c Wells	3	c Bullen
Aylward	0	b Beldam	4	b Clifford
Small, jun.	1	run out	17	ſtumpt out
Crofoer	0	c Bullen	15	run out
Boreman	3	c Bullen	8	c Wells
Ring	12	run out	27	b Clifford
Harris	2	c Beldam	0	b Beldam
Church	2	not out	0	not out
Kenner	3	b Clifford	0	ſtumpt out
Byes	0	Byes	0	
	56		87	

WEST-KENT.

Amherſt	0	c Croſoer	2	b Harris
Hoſmer	0	c ditto	0	b Purchaſe
Crawte	0	run out	0	run out
T. Walker	5	c Harris	15	b Harris
H. Walker	3	b ditto	9	c Croſoer
Brazier	0	b ditto	1	c ditto
Beldam	0	b ditto	9	c ditto
Clifford	4	c Croſoer	8	not out
John Wells	7	b Purchaſe	3	c Purchaſe
Bullen	2	not out	7	c Ring
Palmer	3	b Purchaſe	7	b Purchaſe
Byes	0	Byes	1	
	24		62	

Eaſt-Kent won, 57 runs.

BOURN PADDOCK,
1789.

SURRY, (with Noah Mann) *against KENT.*

AUGUST 11, 12, 13, 14.

SURRY.

	1st inn.		2d inn.	
Ld. Winchelsea	5	b Clifford	2	not out
T. Walker	27	c Crawte		
H. Walker	67	run out		
Beldam	20	c Clifford	0	c Clifford
John Wells	29	c Crosoer	3	not out
James Wells	7	not out		
Souter	59	c Boreman		
Lumpy	0	b Clifford		
Butcher	5	st ditto		
Noah Mann	20	b Boreman		
Ingram	13	c ditto		
Byes	4	Byes	1	
	256		6	

KENT.

	1st inn.		2d inn.	
Sir Peter Burrell	20	c T. Walker	27	run out
Bullen	4	b Beldam	0	b Lumpy
Brazier	37	b Ingram	1	b N. Mann
Aylward	6	b Lumpy	10	c Ingram
Ring	3	c Beldam	14	c Beldam
Pilcher	7	c ditto	6	c John Wells
Boreman	4	b Lumpy	1	not out
Crawte	0	b ditto	39	c N. Mann
Crosoer	38	not out	5	b ditto
Clifford	6	b Lumpy	8	c Beldam
Dean	16	c Ingram	9	b N. Mann
Byes	0	Byes	0	
	141		120	

Surry won, by 9 wickets.

BOURNE PADDOCK,

1789.

HAMPSHIRE, against KENT.

AUGUST 18. 19, 20, 21.

HAMPSHIRE.

	1st inn.		2d inn.	
Ld. Winchelsea	3	b Clifford	2	run out
Louch	4	not out	20	b Bullen
Harris	1	c Crosoer	7	not out
Noah Mann	26	run out	5	c Crosoer
Purchase	59	b Clifford	3	c Bullen
Small, sen.	7	b Bullen	23	b Boreman
Small, jun.	8	c Boreman	29	b Clifford
Freemantle	2	b Clifford	0	c Dean
Taylor	10	b Bullen	6	run out
Scott	9	run out	8	ditto
Stuart	4	c Clifford	0	b Clifford
Byes	2	Byes	3	
	135		106	

KENT.

	1st inn.		2d inn.	
Aylward	37	b Purchase	16	c Taylor
Ring	0	c Harris	7	c Scott
Clifford	12	c Scott	0	b Harris
Bullen	13	b N. Mann	1	b Purchase
Brazier	1	c Scott	13	b Purchase
Crosoer	17	c Harris	8	b ditto
Boreman	1	c Purchase	4	not out
Pilcher	0	b Harris	2	b Harris
Crawte	35	b Taylor	4	c Taylor
Dean	8	b Harris	14	b Harris
Palmer	9	not out	5	b ditto
Byes	4	Byes	1	
	137		75	

Hampshire won, by 29 runs.

This was the last Capital Match played in Bourne Paddock.

SEVENOAKS,
1789.

Hampſhire, (with Ring and Aylward) *againſt all England.*

SEPMEMBER 2, 3, 4, 5.

ALL-ENGLAND.

	1ſt inn.		2d. inn.	
Ld. Winchelſea	2	b N. Mann	0	b Taylor
Beldam	19	not out	14	c Scott
Clifford	5	b Purchaſe	3	b Harris
Bullen	1	c Scott	8	not out
Brazier	4	c Harris	5	c Taylor
John Wells	11	b Purchaſe	39	c Scott
Crawte	6	c Taylor	7	c Harris
Souter	7	b Harris	17	c Small, ſen.
T. Walker	0	b Harris	16	c Aylward
H. Walker	6	hit wicket	10	c Taylor
Lumpy	3	b Purchaſe	0	b Harris
Byes	1	Byes	0	
	65		119	

HAMPSHIRE.

	1ſt inn.		2d inn.	
Aylward	7	b Bullen	13	run out
Ring	1	c H. Walker	38	b Clifford
Harris	2	b Clifford	0	c Crawte
Noah Mann	4	b Bullen	4	c Beldam
Purchaſe	19	b ditto	12	c Crawte
Small, ſen.	13	b Clifford	4	b Clifford
Small, jun.	10	c H. Walker	16	b ditto
Freemantle	3	not out	23	b ditto
Taylor	1	b Bullen	0	b ditto
Scott	0	b ditto	13	c ditto
Foſter	3	b ditto	7	not out
Byes	5	Byes	1	
	68	*N*	131	

Hampſhire won, by 15 runs.

MARY-LE-BONE,
1790.

Eleven left-handed, against Eleven right-handed Players.

MAY 10, 11, 12.

LEFT-HANDED.

	1st inn.		2d inn.	
Harris	4	c Ring	0	b Beldam
Clifford	4	c Beldam	0	b T. Walker
Aylward	30	b ditto	7	b Beldam
Brazier	5	c John Wells	0	c Louch
Crawte *	1	run out	8	c Ring
Souter	39	b Purchafe	0	c Louch
H. Walker	15	c Bullen	15	b Beldam
Freemantle	23	not out	0	c Fennix
Ingram	4	b Purchafe	4	b Beldam
Booker	3	c Taylor	10	c Purchafe
Graham	1	run out	2	not out
Byes	2	Byes	1	
	131		47	

RIGHT-HANDED.

	1st inn.		2d inn.	
Louch	8	b Brazier	1	c Clifford
Bullen	1	not out	0	run out
Purchafe	3	b Harris	2	b Clifford
Taylor	1	b Brazier	8	run out
John Wells	4	c H. Walker	13	b Brazier
Beldam	4	c Ingram	18	b Harris
T. Walker	14	b Clifford	1	run out
Small, fen.	0	c Ingram	4	b Harris
Small, jun.	9	b Harris	19	not out
Ring	21	run out	4	b Harris
Fennix	3	c H. Walker	0	b ditto
Byes	1	Byes	0	
	69		70	

The l. handed won, by 39 runs. *Crawte only throws l. handed.

MARY-LE-BONE,

1790.

LORD WINCHELSEA, against LORD DARNLEY.

JUNE 10, 11, 12.

LORD WINCHELSEA.

	1st inn.		2d inn.	
Ld. Winchelsea	23	b Boreman	2	b Boreman
A. Smith, Esq.	12	c Ring		
Col. Lenox	17	b Brazier	3	not out
Hon. H. Fitzroy	10	not out	2	c Amherst
Louch	6	c Amherst		
Harris	5	c Bullen		
Purchase	1	run out		
Taylor	1	b Brazier		
Small, sen.	33	b Bullen		
Small, jun.	0	b Clifford		
T. Walker	6	c Bullen	12	not out
Byes	5	Byes	0	
	119		19	

LORD DARNLEY.

	1st inn.		2d inn.	
Ld. Darnley	3	c Small, sen.	2	b Purchase
Hon. E. Bligh	4	b Harris	17	c Taylor
Stone	2	not out	0	c ditto
Amherst, Esq.	2	b Harris	0	c Harris
Bullen	11	b Purchase	8	b ditto
Clifford	0	c ditto	8	b ditto
Brazier	2	c Small, jun.	32	b Taylor
Crawte	0	c Taylor	8	b Harris
Aylward	20	c Small, jun.	0	run out
Ring	4	b Purchase	7	b Harris
Boreman	3	c Small, jun.	0	not out
Byes	1	Byes	3	
	52		85	

Lord Winchelsea won, by 8 wickets.

SEVENOAKS,
1790.

Hampſhire, (with Aylward and Ring) *againſt all England.*

JULY 12, 13, 14, 15, 16.

HAMPSHIRE.

	1ſt inn.		2d inn.	
Col. Lenox	15	b Brazier	0	c Clifford
Small, ſen.	24	b Clifford	16	c John Wells
Small, jun.	20	c Burrell	27	b Beldam
Harris	0	not out	1	b Clifford
Taylor	7	b Boreman	8	b ditto
Purchaſe	0	c Clifford	18	b ditto
Freemantle	3	c Souter	25	not out
Annett	18	c Burrell	4	b Bullen
Scott	7	c Beldam	28	b ditto
Aylward	55	c John Wells	10	c Souter
Ring	4	b Clifford	15	b Clifford
Byes	5	Byes	1	
	158		153	

ALL-ENGLAND.

	1ſt inn.		2d inn.	
Sir Peter Burrell	1	b Purchaſe	3	c Lenox
Bullen	2	b ditto	4	c ditto
Brazier	5	c Freemantle	20	c Purchaſe
Boreman	6	c Ring	3	b Harris
Booker	5	not out	14	not out
H. Walker	21	b Purchaſe	41	run out
T. Walker	6	run out	20	c Taylor
John Wells	33	b Taylor	1	run out
Beldam	11	run out	35	c Taylor
Souter	11	c Taylor	17	c Scott
Clifford	4	b Harris	1	c Harris
Byes	1	Byes	2	
	106		161	

Hampſhire won, by 44 runs.

BURLEIGH PARK,
1790.
A MIXED MATCH.
JULY 19, 20, 21.

LORD WINCHELSEA.

	1ſt inn.		2d inn.	
Ld. Winchelſea	23	c Clifford	1	b Taylor
Ld. Darnley	4	c Purchaſe	10	ſtumpt out
Louch	8	c Butcher	17	c Butcher
H. Walker	0	c Taylor	1	c Taylor
T. Walker	31	c ditto	16	b Purchaſe
John Wells	8	b Purchaſe	21	c Small, jun.
Beldam	0	hit wicket	0	c ditto
Souter	8	run out	19	b Purchaſe
Bullen	6	not out	8	b ditto
Brazier	4	b Clifford	1	b ditto
Boreman	0	c Small, ſen.	6	not out
Byes	0	Byes	3	
	92		103	

MR. A. SMITH.

	1ſt inn.		2d inn.	
A. Smith, Eſq.	15	not out	0	
Butcher	1	b Brazier	1	b Bullen
Anguiſh	0	c Boreman		
Small, ſen.	0	b Brazier		
Small, jun.	9	b Beldam	30	not out
Purchaſe	3	c ditto		
Taylor	36	run out		
Clifford	4	c Louch		
Freemantle	0	run out	1	b Bullen
Aylward	36	c John Wells	5	c John Wells
Ring	24	c Beldam	24	not out
Byes	7	Byes	0	
	135		61	

Mr. A. Smith won, by 7 wickets.

PERRAM-DOWNS,
1790.
Sir HORACE MANN, against Mr. A. SMITH.
JULY 27, 28. 29.

SIR HORACE MANN.

	1st inn.		2d inn.	
Ld. Darnley	5	b Purchase	3	b Taylor
Amherst, Esq.	18	b Beldam	11	c Beldam
Butcher	1	c H. Walker	13	not out
Freemantle	26	c Beldam	0	b Beldam
Clifford	10	b ditto	1	b Taylor
Bullen	10	b Purchase	0	b T. Walker
Boxall	6	not out	0	c John Wells
Aylward	0	c Taylor	29	b Taylor
Ring	9	c Beldam	8	b Beldam
White	6	b Purchase	9	b T. Walker
Crawte	0	c John Wells	31	c ditto
Byes	0	Byes	0	
	91		96	

MR. A. SMITH.

	1st inn.		2d inn.	
Ld. Winchelsea	0	b Bullen	9	c Amherst
A. Smith, Esq.	0	b Clifford	4	b Bullen
Louch	25	not out	0	b Clifford
Anguish	9	run out	2	c Amherst
John Wells	11	b Clifford		
Purchase	0	run out	19	not out
Taylor	26	c Amherst		
Beldam	60	b Ld. Darnley		
H. Walker	15	b Clifford		
T. Walker	2	b ditto	1	not out
Small, jun.	4	b Bullen		
Byes	0	Byes	1	
	152		36	

Mr. A. Smith won, by 6 wickets.

WINDMILL DOWNS,

1790.

A MIXED MATCH.

AUGUST 4, 5, 6, 7.

LORD DARNLEY.

	1ſt inn.		2d inn.	
Ld. Darnley	7	c Souter	0	b Bullen
A. Smith, Eſq.	2	b Beldam	6	b ditto
French	0	b Bullen	1	not out
Small, ſen.	12	b Beldam	19	run out
Small, jun.	39	c Brazier	5	c H. Walker
Aylward	9	b Beldam	6	b Beldam
Ring	68	b Bullen	13	b ditto
Purchaſe	73	b Brazier	13	b Bullen
Clifford	34	c Brazier	5	c John Wells
Taylor	14	b Bullen	6	b Beldam
Freemantle	13	not out	32	c H. Walker
Byes	7	Byes	2	
	278		108	

LORD WINCHELSEA.

	1ſt inn.		2d inn.	
Ld. Winchelſea	19	c Aylward	19	b Clifford
Louch	1	b Ld. Darnley	8	b Purchaſe
John Wells	5	c Taylor	3	c Small, jun.
Beldam	54	c Smith	11	b Purchaſe
T. Walker	0	b Purchaſe	5	b Clifford
H. Walker	9	run out	0	b ditto
Souter	0	b Clifford	12	c Small, ſen.
Crawte	22	b Ld. Darnley	3	c French
Brazier	1	b ditto	19	not out
Bullen	0	b Taylor	0	c Small, ſen.
Butcher	0	not out	4	c ditto
Byes	5	Byes	1	
	116		85	

Lord Darnley won, by 185 runs.

MARY-LE-BONE,

1790.

Hampshire, against All England, (with 4 Gentlemen on each side)

AUGUST 30, 31.

HAMPSHIRE.

	1st inn.		2d inn.	
Ld. Winchelsea	15	st Clifford		
Ld. Darnley	1	b Beldam		
Dehaney	0	b ditto		
Louch	6	b T. Walker		
Harris	10	not out		
Purchase	0	run out		
Taylor	31	b Clifford		
Small, sen.	1	run out		
Small, jun.	51	c H. Walker	32	not out
Freemantle	5	b Clifford		
Scott	43	c John Wells	44	not out
Byes	2	Byes	3	
	165		79	

ALL-ENGLAND.

	1st inn.		2d inn.	
Col. Lenox	0	c Taylor	0	b Harris
Anguish	0	b Harris	11	b ditto
Hon. E. Capell	19	c Louch	0	c Purchase
Graham	5	not out	3	not out
Clifford	7	c Small, sen.	0	c Purchase
Beldam	31	b Purchase	3	b Harris
H. Walker	20	c Ld. Winchelsea	3	b ditto
T. Walker	60	b Harris	0	b ditto
John Wells	9	c Taylor	0	c Taylor
Aylward	14	b Harris	27	b ditto
Bullen	11	b ditto	15	b Harris
Byes	1	Byes	4	
	177		66	

Hampshire won, by 10 wickets.

FINIS.

Errata. Page 31, for 1779, read 1778.]

[Printed by W. Epps, Rochester.